Elizabeth Grinnell

John and I and the Church

Elizabeth Grinnell

John and I and the Church

ISBN/EAN: 9783337003500

Printed in Europe, USA, Canada, Australia, Japan

Cover: Foto ©ninafisch / pixelio.de

More available books at **www.hansebooks.com**

WHEN HE ROSE TO SPEAK HE WAVED HIS HANDKERCHIEF.

John and I and the Church

BY

Elizabeth Grinnell

AUTHOR OF "HOW JOHN AND I BROUGHT UP THE CHILD"

*Who builds a church to God, and not to fame,
Will never mark the marble with his name*
POPE, EPISTLE III, LINE 285

Illustrated

New York   Chicago   Toronto
Fleming H. Revell Company
mdcccxcvii

COPYRIGHT
FLEMING H. REVELL COMPANY
1897

CONTENTS.

CHAPTER		PAGE
I	The Church Outgrows John	7
II	The Church Has a Boom	15
III	The Church Gives us a Pound Party and a Missionary Box	22
IV	John's Views of Church Debt	30
V	The Pew-System as it was Worked in Our Church	36
VI	Parting Scenes	41
VII	John's Farewell Sermon	47
VIII	John Finds a New Field	55
IX	At Sunrise Park	64
X	A Church Reception	70
XI	We Receive Calls	78
XII	I Begin to Look Like a Minister's Wife	84
XIII	My Neighbors Stop Borrowing	92
XIV	Abijah Noseworthy's Wild Oats	97
XV	Silas Coombs and Death-Bed Scenes	103
XVI	The Church Has a Revival	111
XVII	Church Gossip	122
XVIII	At the Women's Meeting	128
XIX	Was it a Foundling?	140
XX	John Did Not Kiss Mrs. Black's Little Girl	150
XXI	A Proposal of Marriage	156
XXII	I Attend Some Other Churches	166
XXIII	Election and Reprobation	173
XXIV	The Tuttle Family	178
XXV	Company to Dinner	188
XXVI	Earth to Earth, Ashes to Ashes, Dust to Dust, in Sure and Certain Hope of the Resurrection	196

LIST OF ILLUSTRATIONS.

	PAGE
HE COULD ALMOST WISH THE LITTLE FLOCK HAD NEVER OUTGROWN THE DRUG-STORE HALL	9
I LAID THE THINGS ALL OUT IN ARRAY ON THE PARLOR SOFA	28
CHURCH-DEBT COMMITTEES CALL	34
MRS. JONES SHOWS HER PERTURBATION	38
CONVERSING AWHILE WITH HIS NEW CONSTITUENCY	73
MOTHER WANTS TO BORROW SOME OF THE MORNING'S MILK	82
WHEN HE ROSE TO SPEAK, HE WAVED HIS HANDKERCHIEF	98
JOHN HELD THE LIGHT WHILE FRANK OVERMAN WENT OVER THE RIVER	110
IT WAS AS IF HE WERE "TAKING STOCK"	115
TELLING THE CHILDREN STORIES WHILE SHE CLEANED THEM UP AND MADE MRS. TUTTLE COMFORTABLE	184

CHAPTER I

The Church Outgrows John

The little church at Hope Valley Corners outgrew John. It had been John's first charge. In fact there was no church at all in Hope Valley when John preached his first sermon in the little hall, 15x20, above the one drug store in the village.

John was not a "fledgling," so to speak, when he commenced his ministry. He had passed early youth before he had ever announced a text, or attempted to preach, save as he held an occasional service in the schoolhouse. He often declared that he was not prepared to "take a charge" until he had spent some years in observation; although he was urged to do so before the ink of his graduating thesis was dry, or he had learned that sympathy is born of experience. He firmly declined, preferring to "teach school," he said, "until I have become intimate with human nature and its common needs." He often says to me that "with the tearing down of the little country schoolhouse is passing away the best opportunity of developing the perceptions of doctor, lawyer, or minister."

The Church Outgrows John

When he went to preach in Hope Valley there was little salary attached to the "call." Enough, however, for us two and the baby to live upon as comfortably as the majority of people about us. To be sure there were a few who were "well to do," living in houses rather pretentious, and dressing expensively. One or two of these favored of fortune belonged to our church, or rather to the little hall above the drug store.

It was not long before the small room was crowded. More chairs were brought—not bought. There was little to contribute to the church save chairs and a few lamps. Rents were low—and so was the minister's pay. As to the chairs being brought, John often says that he wishes large churches were furnished in that way. There is a personal satisfaction in providing seats for strangers, just as you would draw the chairs up to the fire in your own house and bid anyone who happened to drop in "feel at home." Of course, in general church expenses the seating usually comes in, but we miss the satisfaction of a personal interest in those who occupy the pews. One cannot look about and say to himself, "I am glad I brought that chair, for there is Mr. Brotherly-love, or Mr. Timorous sitting in it. I believe I shall bring another."

In less than a year there was not even standing-room around John. The congregation sat

HE COULD ALMOST WISH THE LITTLE FLOCK HAD
NEVER OUTGROWN THE DRUG-STORE HALL.

The Church Outgrows John

or stood so close to him that, undemonstrative as he was, he could not point in the direction of Jerusalem, nor pronounce the benediction without touching the heads of those about him. He has often remarked to me that "hearts were near, as well," and he could almost wish that, for its own sake, the little flock had never outgrown the small dimensions of the drug=store hall. Fill the small "upper rooms," a score of them, rather than crowd into one large house. It is easier to "continue with one accord" in such places; there is less danger of rivalry and worldliness and unsympathy. Where a congregation touches elbows in a Sabbath service, heart more easily meets heart; hence, more love.

John was intimate with every one of his flock, and with a great many who were not of his flock. He was genial, persuasive, and free in manner. He did not wear a "ministerial moral garb." The young folks did not stop laughing when they saw him coming, nor did their elders drop business perplexities and assume a spiritual air. He was plain=spoken; calm, though emphatic in delivery.

And he was extremely simple, if to be simple is to be understood. He never reverted to the "Hebrew text," nor to the "Greek translation." He was preaching, he said, "to a common people who read a common Bible; and he would not re-

The Church Outgrows John

fer to a possible mistake in that Bible, lest a doubt in the validity of one passage might father doubts in the whole. There are plenty of texts," he said, "which need no display of my small knowledge of Greek and Hebrew, and from these I can feed the flock. Many a man has been taught his first lessons in skepticism from the pulpit."

When the time came that the little hall could hold no more, and others were waiting outside, the question of a new building was discussed. John suggested that services might be held in some of the schoolhouses, and mentioned the names of several ministers who could preach in them. But our people had set their hearts on a new church, and it did not take long to raise a thousand dollars to build one. It was paid for when it was completed, and not left to be paid for after it was finished. It would hold two hundred, and there was some chair-room besides. It was comfortably furnished with a plain carpet and cushioned seats, a sweet-toned organ, and had a vestry for the use of the Sunday-school. The ceiling was dome-shaped and finished in natural wood. There is a suggestion of the sky, or of heaven itself in a dome, that is impossible in a square ceiling, or even in one of frescoed corners and pinnacles—a hint that boundary lines are far distant; a possibility of stars somewhere.

The Church Outgrows John

The modest belfry was just high enough to accommodate a clear-voiced bell, the gift of a bereaved wife whose husband had sung in the choir. "The bell should ring," she said, "in place of the voice that was silent." The whole edifice was a model of neatness and consistency. John's salary was raised a trifle to correspond with his increased duties, for the work widened with more membership.

It was the first time in our married life when we could lay up a small sum as we went along. John was "very thankful for it all," he said. John always gave his first thought to his family. That seems a strange thing to say of a minister. John had no desire to amass wealth nor to make his calling a stepladder to riches, but he says that "any man, a minister not excepted, who provides not for his own house, has denied the faith and is worse, in this respect, than an infidel."

"A man should honor God by honoring his family, God's best gift to any man."

"Why, John," I would say, "does it not read, 'Seek ye first the kingdom of God and all these things shall be added?' Of course we are to infer from this that a Christian believer, especially a minister, ought not to think anything about the needs of to-morrow, but be all the time seeking the kingdom. If he is poor, or even in

The Church Outgrows John

distress, it is a sign that he has been very faithful."

John smiled and kissed the baby just as if I had made no remark at all. Then he spoke, as if to the little one: "We have sought the kingdom, my child, and if God does not keep His word by adding these things, the fault must be our own. God is faithful; we must be faithful as well, nor stand in the way of His fulfilling His part of the contract. He does not say that in spite of our carelessness or thriftlessness or waste or even the misconception of His Word 'all these things shall be added.' 'He knoweth that ye have need of these things,' home and clothes and education and means of culture and gold wherewith to help them who have not yet sought the kingdom. Of more value is the kingdom than all these things; but when once it is found, why go on seeking it instead of making ourselves fit subjects for that kingdom?"

"Yes, but John," I said, "what does it say about the lilies and the birds being clothed and fed? I was taught that we must be like them and take no thought; that certainly is what the Bible says."

"It is the 'thought,' the fretting, the borrowing trouble, the useless presentiments of poverty, that the Lord would have us avoid. There

The Church Outgrows John

are the pinching and the saving, the depriving of oneself and family of the comforts of to-day, in order to save a greater sum for to-morrow. It is the dread of the poorhouse which haunts some men in the face of affluence. Are ye not better than the birds and lilies? Have ye not perception and ability and judgment and thrift and energy and trust in God? If He clothe them who have no storehouses or barns will He not fill our granaries? I believe it is not the Father's will that there be a pauper in the Christian church. The cattle upon a thousand hills are His; let the church see to it that the markets are also His."

The little new church thrived. There were no poor among its members. By "poor" I mean there were no collections taken up for anybody. "Love is the fulfilling of the law," John preached. "If we keep love, we keep the law, and *vice versa*. By keeping love we keep fellowship, and fellowship is what is needed in the church more than anything else. Do good unto all men, especially to them of the household of faith. This is the principle of all the fraternal orders. Secret societies, as a rule, embody this principle, and they have stolen it from the church who has herself neglected the command. If church members could find in the church that fraternity, aid, fellowship, which are offered

The Church Outgrows John

and obtained elsewhere, there would cease to be heard the lament that Christain men seek the secret order. The church needs a 'grip' of her own. Give it to the unfortunate; to the man who has failed; to him who, for some unaccountable reason, is no manager, a poor provider. Give it to the backslider, to the successful man, to the rich, and to the poor. If there is a blacksmith in the church, take your horses to his shop to be shod. The shoes will last as long as if put on by some one outside the church. If there is a church member who is a grocer, buy your tea and flour of him, and your clothes of his cousin, the merchant. If you have a doctor or a lawyer who stands well in his profession, give him no time to practice outside the church. If you need a house-girl, or a field-hand, make your selection from the church. And the church will see to it that its members 'take no thought for to-morrow.' When the church becomes a fraternal order—and more than this, an insurance company—individual members will have as little anxiety about the future as the birds and the lilies have."

Yes, indeed, the little church thrived, as I said. But there came a change. If there had not, then I should never have written this story.

CHAPTER II

The Church has a Boom

Yes, our little church had a boom. It was like a devastating cyclone, sweeping away fellowship and humility and peace and content. Hope Valley Corners changed its name to New Rome City--and a city it became in a flash. In less than a year after the first corner-lot was sold for a fabulous sum, there were built grand churches and residences and magnificent halls. Architecture became the mania. Our little meeting-house was moved from the old site to the outer circumference of the city. The lot upon which it had stood was wanted by the owner for a bank; and besides, the house itself was not suitable from the standpoint of boom times. Not but that it was large enough, but it had "no style."

Several of our church members became suddenly rich—or were considered so, which is about the same thing—and it dawned upon our people that we must have a new building.

John suggested that we build a sort of tabernacle, or people's church—a "God's House," which should stand for no particular creed; a

The Church has a Boom

landmark on the road to heaven. It was John's dream to do away with creed and sect. But our people were suddenly bent upon an edifice of denominational caste; nothing else would satisfy them. They were also determined to rival their fellow churches—not in goodness and meekness and love and helpfulness and the other spiritual graces, but in the splendor of their sanctuary.

"Oh, the hollowness of it all," John said, "the worldliness; the church making of herself a side-show in Vanity Fair!" The true house is within us; architecture cannot wall it in, nor masonry deceive as to the true character of it.

When the committee canvassed the flock for funds, the ready cash fell far short of the estimated cost. There were "subscriptions," however, dependent upon sales, and pocketfuls upon pocketfuls of promises. John warned the committee, lovingly at first; firmly, and fairly protesting, at last, but to no avail. There were some that stood with him, but the majority ruled in the matter, and the new church was contracted for. In the end it was twenty thousand dollars in debt.

What a change came over the members, or the most of them! They kept up the show of worship, but the spirit of it was not there.

In the strife for wealth consequent upon the boom, brother deceived brother, and each sought

The Church has a Boom

to outwit the other in bargain and sale. To get the best in a business transaction, in short, to defraud, was a common thing. But these men went to church and sat upon their unpaid-for velvet cushions and sang and joined in the Lord's Prayer and—oh, for the shame of it!—they even took the bread and wine. Judas, one out of twelve, betrayed the Lord with a kiss—there was scarcely one out of twelve in our church who did not put his lips to the sacrament, go out among his fellows, and deny his Lord!

To keep up appearances, John's salary was raised to double what it had been. But when it came to the quarterly payment it actually fell far short of the old stipend. The amount stipulated was published, however, in true boom style; and John, like a corner-lot, was rated at a fictitious value. Other churches paid high salaries, or published high salaries, and ours was not to be outdone.

As I said in the first place, the church outgrew John. And yet everybody loved John. He preached the same simple, plain sermons which he had always preached. Coming from anybody but John they would not have been tolerated. Nothing else was expected from him; he was too sincere to be, or seem other than he was. Yet we could see that he did not always please.

The Church has a Boom

A good many rich people joined the church, by letter and otherwise, naturally enough; it was so much more stylish than any of the others. Some of the more common members, who did not care for style, quietly withdrew to smaller churches. I do not mean to say that rich men, as we found them, were always hollow and artificial when it came to actual facts. But wealth, as a rule, does seek its kind; hence we find caste. I have noticed that the little plain churches are filled with little plain people, for no other reason, perhaps, than that little fish are in little pools; they feel more at home. It is as much caste on the part of the poor as on the part of the rich. They will separate, these on this side and those on that. I wish it were not so, and yet I see no way of changing the order, save to adopt a church garb or uniform. I think dress does more than anything else to separate the rich from the poor in the house of God.

After a while, "owing to circumstances over which we had no control," we were actually in need of the necessaries of life, though we did not mention it. Little by little we used our savings which we had laid by when John preached in the old church before the boom. We felt sorry, but John felt sorrier for his people. They had a great burden to bear. They

The Church has a Boom

must keep up appearances in the new church. The interest on the debt was high, and there were improvements constantly to be made. Subscribers to the cost of it all moved away, or for other reasons failed to keep their word.

I had one consolation in our trouble, for, as I said, "everybody loved John." I believed that it was only from necessity that they failed to pay him, or hinted that he could not be retained another year. This is what they said, and why should I doubt their word, especially when they prefaced their tears by assuring me how much they "loved John?" "The necessities of the case," they said, "the necessities of the case demand a change."

In some vague way I was impressed with their sincerity, and I wish I had never come to disbelieve them.

After a while we came to understand. The church wanted a preacher with a "record" behind him like a trotting-horse or a fast-time engine. One who had shone in New York or London or Chicago, as pastor of some "tony" church; one who would "cover a multitude of sins," especially such trifling sins as beset our church. They wanted a minister whose discourses would be flowery and sparkling with imagination; who would choose a text occasionally from somewhere outside of the Bible, and

The Church has a Boom

also indulge in "lovely quotations from the poets."

Now John quoted poetry, but his was not the sort to please under the circumstances. Taste, in our church, had become suddenly esthetic. Then, too, our people thought that a minister who had traveled would be "drawing." Lectures on foreign lands and customs are so "taking" on Sunday evenings, especially in a popular church. They could postpone the saving of the world and the new birth of individuals until the church debt was paid.

Pending a call to someone else, John preached on, and it was not known outside that it was his last year. That last year was a hard one for us. The sense of being wronged by brethren; indignation at insults degrading to us and to the name of religion; the acceptance of charity in the place of justice, and alms in lieu of our rights—all this made me, at least, dissatisfied.

I would have had John leave at once and let the church "hoe its own row," but John said, "No." He would stay as long as they wanted him, and he might keep them from greater mistakes. The Spirit of the Master was more at home with John than with me.

Besides all this moral burden our physical want was fast bordering on distress. This was

The Church has a Boom

soon known to enough of our friends if they had but felt the exigencies of it. It is hard to excuse this lack of justice on the part of our church. A boom in any church or city destroys moral susceptibilities. Demands having legal claims behind them are considered first. Such demands were many and pressing in our town and on our people. They did not mean to rob John, nor to use for other purposes the money that was his. They forgot their contract with him and, had they stopped to think, they would have known he would not press his claim in law. He was at their mercy. "Personal business cares and church liabilities" were their excuses, though no excuse was made to John. The subject was avoided.

CHAPTER III

The Church Gives Us a Pound Party and a Missionary Box

Some trifling incidents, by way of doubtful apology, occurred about this time, which did not mend matters a great deal. The members strove hard, in their way, to keep up a show of good feeling. They attempted to smooth the irregularities of the way by methods well known to the church at large. For instance, one evening, without previous announcement to us, they came to our house in a body, cheerful to hilarity. They constituted what is termed a "pound party" and spent the evening in forced good nature. They brought flour, and bacon, and sugar, and dried apples, and potatoes, and tea, and canned salmon, and pickles, and yeast, and bologna sausage, and cheese, and bread, and pie, and cake. Just as relief committees carry baskets of supplies to the destitute.

Now we were well-nigh destitute, to be sure, but that was the fault of these very people. They owed John, and they took this way of paying the debt. It was like saying, "God bless

A Pound Party

you," to one's grocer and butcher and hired girl, and expecting them to smile and take the will for the deed, and so consider the account square.

John and I tried to be hospitable and to join in the merrymaking, but we were too much taken by surprise to act our part to perfection. I suppose we were considered ungrateful. Evidently John was expected to make sweet and witty speeches over the packages and bags of provisions, but if he had such a thought as to say, "For what we receive make us truly thankful," he broke down before he began. We would so much rather have had the money which the things cost in the first place, little as it was.

It had now been five months since John had received a dollar. I was overworked with such duties as I had hired done before, and there were two babies—blessed babies!—to nurse. I do not know that I ever saw John really indignant but once that year, and that was not personal resentment, I am sure, but abhorrence of the principle. He overheard a remark which one lady made to another, signifying that "ministers owe it to their churches to have small families."

John preached a sermon the following Sunday on the text, "Lo, children are a heritage of the Lord, and the fruit of the womb is his reward."

A Pound Party

He dwelt particularly upon the word "heritage" as meaning "an estate bequeathed, real property, or personal ownership of what is valuable." "Ill-health, lonely and childless old age, remorse, the sting of memory, the sharp reproach of a thousand things, all combine to form a heritage such as, though terrible, is entailed upon modern regulators of families."

It was one of his plainest sermons, striking at the root of domestic evils, and laying bare the sins of parental responsibility, until those of his hearers whose faces did not burn, turned pale with an unwonted sense of guilt: "Woman has been the cause of her own misery ever since Eve transgressed. Some men call the story of Eden a myth. Be that as it may, woman's own hand has pressed to her lips the bitter fruit of all ages, although she still has little excuse and lays the fault to her 'constitution' or to her 'sphere,' as Eve laid it to the serpent. She plots and conspires against human life in the days of her youth, and when age and sorrow whiten her hair she weeps that the cell of the murderer is never empty. She herself built the scaffold for her posterity while they were yet unborn, and she is chilled to the heart at last by her own deeds." John said to me afterward that that sermon had been on his mind for a

A Pound Party

long while, and that the feeling of years had found expression.

"But John," I said, "I am afraid you were too plain, especially as there were a good many really delicate ladies present who looked hurt and shocked at what you said. Society demands reticence upon certain points, and you know, John, one should not offend real refinement."

John made me no reply, and I did not know until years afterward that it was one of those same "delicate ladies" to whom I had referred who had made the remark, in John's hearing, that "ministers owe it to their churches to have small families."

It was not long after the "pound party" that a box was left at our door directed to John, "freight payable on delivery." We managed to pay the bill by borrowing from the children's little tin banks, we not being flush of money, and we wondered what it could be that was in the box.

We opened it, breathless, thinking of far-away friends to whom we had no reason to look for gifts. It would take a good while for me to run through with the list. It was a collection of second-hand raiment solicited for destitute ministers and retired missionaries. How it

A Pound Party

came to be sent to us we never knew, but probably it, like the pound party, came of good intentions.

There were shirts and hose for John, worn thin and needing repairs. There was an overcoat, which might have come over with the Pilgrim Fathers, so antiquated and threadbare it was; besides, it was made to fit a man twice John's size. Then there were some old dresses with the buttons and trimmings ripped off; some white cotton skirts with ragged lace on the bottom, and two old bonnets; some gloves with the fingers cut off, suggesting "mitts," and a parasol. There were some frayed old blankets, too, through whose thin middle I could distinctly see John's face as I held them up before him and the window.

We had endured much, but this swelled the torrent of my feelings beyond high=water mark. The stream gushed with the impetus of a tide in springtime when the snow is melting, and I did not even try to control the flood.

To stand by and see John insulted like this! John, who was the height of a man above every other man in the community in what best makes a man! John, who could have commanded thousands in either of the professions, but who chose to preach the Gospel as the best means of restoring a sick world!—all this for a

A Pound Party

sum that at its best only meant comfortable support. Oh, I was indignant!

"What are ministers made of," I exclaimed, "that they and their families should be insulted in this way? Ministers who are earning an honest living if the church itself, clothed in scarlet and fine linen, would but pay its debts! Ministers whose sense of personal independence is as natural and therefore as right as that of any other man! Who ever thinks of meeting his obligations at the bank with old clothes? Who pays his lawyer's fees with second-hand coats and stockings, and who meets his grocers' claims with pound parties? Who but a minister would see his wife rigged out in other women's finery?" Thus I went on until I was ashamed of my temper, and John said I "mustn't scold."

He took up the babies, one on either shoulder, and marched around the room singing "Old Hundred" as only John can sing it. After a while I laughed as heartily as I had scolded—and John joined in, the whole thing was so ludicrous.

John says "when a man laughs at trouble the trouble laughs too and turns into a sprite to fly away." I would have had John wear the Pilgrim Father overcoat to church, but he wouldn't. I did what was almost as bad, though,

A Pound Party

and John didn't object. I laid the things all out in array on the parlor sofa and showed them to everybody that came in, saying: "See what a present came to us the other day!" It was wonderful, the amount of good healthy color that found its way into the cheeks of my callers. And I was as unconscious of their embarrassment as could be, of course; indeed, I was never in better spirits. John said the affair was worth what it cost for its effect upon me. It was like some unpalatable medicine toning me up after a year's moral illness.

It was not long afterward that we read in the daily paper a paragraph something like this: "It is with profound regret that we learn of the resignation of the Rev. John ———, pastor of the First Street Church, New Rome City. He has served that body for five years, during which time he has given entire satisfaction. He leaves a salary of two thousand dollars and a warm-hearted people. Failing health is the cause of his resignation."

John and I looked at each other in consternation. John's health was perfect. He had never had "a sick day in his life," as the saying is. And John never "resigned." Why this story was ever concocted I leave it with the officers of the First Street Church to ex-

I LAID THE THINGS ALL OUT IN ARRAY ON THE
PARLOR SOFA.

A Pound Party

plain. Was it for John's sake or their own that they covered the real truth?

John was astonished. He did not say a word, but I knew he was thinking of the church. Visions of the old days in Hope Valley came to him, when the congregation touched elbows and hearts in the little drug=store hall. He would have helped his people over this last hill, Difficulty, though his own feet were torn in the ascent.

CHAPTER IV
John's Views of Church Debt

As the time drew near when John must preach his farewell sermon, I felt bad. I didn't let John know it, though. I would not add a crushed straw to his heavy load. John himself was not sad—that is, not gloomy. He has always said that no personal trial, save death and sin, ought to make a Christian sad—not even the loss of all his property.

I often told him that "the natural temperament has everything to do with it."

"Not everything," he would answer. "Man is born ignorant and helpless. Knowledge and self-reliance are foreign to the child and must be grafted upon him. Cheerfulness should be grafted into him also, and serenity. The more faith grows, the more ought good cheer to grow. Peace is only another word for happiness."

One of John's favorite quotations is this: "Wisdom's ways are ways of pleasantness." He says: "The more wisdom, the more pleasantness, but men neglect the one in striving for the other; growing morose and unsociable and

John's Views of Church Debt

self-absorbed in the determination to be wise, forgetting that real wisdom only travels in pleasant ways."

St. Paul said of his church: "I know that after my departing shall grievous wolves enter in among you not sparing the flock." In the case of our church the "grievous wolves" had already entered. Looking back over it all now, I can see how gradually they had crept in, stealthily creeping through the openings in the wall, slily finding a way through the partly open gate, making no disturbance, and attacking no one in the guise of a wolf.

Greed was the first to enter. Its coming was so sudden that it was running all around among the flock before the sheep recognized it. In a short while it had grown so familiar, and seemed so gentle, that the sheep ceased to flee from it, but allowed it to feed in the very best part of the pasture. The Lord knew human nature best when He said: "It is easier for a camel to go through the eye of a needle than for a rich man to enter into the kingdom." Rich men, like the camel, have a hump on the back, and they must stoop low or graze the hump. Unlike the camel, however, the rich man is not used to stooping; he will enter upright, grasping his hump with both hands and never letting go, unless perchance some fellow-

John's Views of Church Debt

traveler, forcing his way amid the throng, knocks it off. The trouble is not with the hump. The camel goes in before the rich man because he kneels.

In the church are men who seek for riches day and night; men upon whom riches are thrust by inheritance, or by sudden rise in values, and men who imagine they have riches. These last are the worst in church or state, for, counting on what they expect, they multiply what they do possess beyond reason. They build mansions, paying for them in promises at a rate of interest as enormous as the promises; and, to be consistent, they build churches as luxurious as their homes, paying for them also in promises. Then "My Father's House is a house of merchandise," indeed. In it the white doves of peace and brotherly love are sold for a farthing's worth of pretension.

John said that in those years he had had his first experience in church debt, and he would never have a second. "Debt," he said, "is a millstone around the neck of the church and of every individual member, though, sooner or later, by dint of hard struggles, they nearly always emerge and limp disabled up the bank, dripping with the tide of jealousy and discontent."

There are men, usually worn-out ministers,

John's Views of Church Debt

whose one talent lies in paying off church debts. They are sent for far and near like a quack doctor, and they hold meetings and give "chalk talks" and emblazon blackboards with figures, doing sums for pupils already far advanced in "partial payments." There is never a word said about the calamity of church debt The speaker smiles perpetually, and before they know it all his auditors are smiling. Four per cent. of the debt is wiped out in an hour and the "talented man" hies him to other fields to smile again.

He ought to weep. If he would but give his attention to warding off church debts instead of paying them off he would do the kingdom of God a greater favor. "Owe no man anything but to love one another." What a preface to church creeds this would be!

Once in debt, a church is never on the old footing. There are bitter losses to bear, fortunes of good feeling squandered in a day, and good feeling is scarcer and more precious than gold.

Each thinks his church=fellow should pay more than he does. Another murmurs because in his stress of circumstances he is forced or expected to pay anything. Yet another absolutely refuses to pay any part of a debt which he had "no hand in contracting."

John's Views of Church Debt

"Church=debt committees" call at irregular times upon the members to urge the payment of a sum "to meet at least the interest on the debt." Usually the members of the committee are rich, but they are loath to meet more than they can possibly help of the obligation. "Besides," they argue, "it is right for each and all to bear a part." They drive up to the door of the delinquent member, shake hands stiffly, smile sadly, inquire after the family with enforced interest, say something as to the weather or town prospects, and hesitate a good while before getting at the business in hand.

The host knows by intuition the errand of his visitor and helps him not out of his embarrassment by so much as a distant allusion to the subject in both minds. Does he not know that he would never have received a call from his church brother but for the fact that the brother wants gold? When, at length, the subject is approached, and the brother called upon yields his pittance, there is no fellow=feeling, unless it be one of hardness. The committeeman thinks that the amount given should have exceeded the actual gift, and the other wishes he "hadn't given anything." So do "grievous wolves" spoil the flock.

Oh, John and I grew intimate with the whole aspect of church debt during those years, and

CHURCH-DEBT COMMITTEE'S CALL.

John's Views of Church Debt

John declared he would never preach for a congregation that assumed such a burden. He used to say that "if all ministers would bind themselves to such a resolve, church debt would soon be a feature of the dark ages in church history."

CHAPTER V

The Pew System as it was Worked in Our Church

I think that of all the sad consequences of church debt, that was the saddest which compelled the pew system. It was so hard to make collections that the officers declared themselves in favor of renting the pews. John pleaded with them to no avail. Once made desperate by church debt, everything was subservient to its demands. So the pews were sold.

There was not any church auction proper, but the pews were sold to the highest bidder in a quiet way. An imaginary line was drawn around the auditorium. In this circle pews were worth three hundred; in that, one hundred and fifty; in the other, seventy-five; and so on down, until far back under the gallery there was no price attached.

All this, of course, encouraged church caste. There were first-class, second-class, and third-class members, and "strays." I do not mean to say that there was a visible label or tag to each, but a stranger could have guessed where the line of demarcation was drawn.

The Pew System

The "four hundred" had the best seats, right in front of the pulpit, in the middle of the beautiful house. Overhead the cherubs and mighty angels flying through imaginary space poised exactly above them.

Under solitary frescoed stars, without guardian angels, sat the second-class members. Above them was the plainer slope of the arching dome.

There were four ushers appointed to seat the congregation. Two of these were for the middle section, or first-class neighborhood, and were selected from the four hundred's own number. They took care to seat the splendidly dressed owners of the front pews who, coming early or late, were sure to find their seats unoccupied. That is, they *hardly ever* found them occupied. The ushers, who understood their business, kept an eye on the church doors, and when strangers appeared who had the unmistakable air of aristocracy they were ushered down to the proper neighborhood. There was cheerful room made for such.

The other two ushers were for the second and third-class sections.

John refused a seat for his own family which was courteously tendered to us in the middle, or first-class circle. We preferred to sit well back under the gallery. That suited me well enough, for I was silently studying human nature as

The Pew System

one finds it in church. The whole panorama glides before me now after the lapse of so many years, and nobody will guess whom I mean if I speak their names right out.

In walks neighbor Smith followed by his wife and children, confidently expecting to find their own pew empty and ready for them. They pause at the entrance to find it already occupied. Each of the family casts a questioning glance up and down the pew, as much as to say, "This is our seat. How came you in it?" The embarrassed occupants try to make room for the real owners of the pew, but the Smith's walk away to some other locality, looking askance at the usher whose fault has brought all this trouble. The usher himself is embarrassed. He had to seat the strangers somewhere, or tell them to go on to the next church.

Mrs. Jones comes down the aisle and shows her perturbation so emphatically at finding strangers in her pew that the strangers gather up their shawls and hats and step politely out. Mrs. Jones settles herself comfortably in the seat just vacated. Isn't it her pew, and hasn't she paid a good round sum for it?

Mr. and Mrs. Brown are looking over the floor plan of the house, pinned in place on the outer door of the vestibule. The prices of the pews are plainly marked. Mr. Brown is just a com-

MRS. JONES SHOWS HER PERTURBATION.

The Pew System

mon man, is not rich, pays his debts, and goes to church. There is quite a family of children and they have always filled a whole seat before the pew system had its day. Mr. and Mrs. Brown read the price of the sittings and one says, with a sigh, "Well, I guess three sittings will do for us. We needn't all come to church at the same time, and twenty-five dollars is all we are able to pay just now." Not one of the church officers ever says to Mr. Brown, "Why don't you bring the whole family? Come right in and feel at home. There's room enough; we want the whole of you here." If the officers say anything, it is in a side whisper to the effect that "if Mr. Brown wants more room he can rent the whole pew."

And this is the church of Christ!

John says there always has been an inclination in the human heart to get the best seat. For instance, there was the Mother of Zebedee's children. She wanted her two sons to have front seats in the church of the New Jerusalem. So she came to Jesus, thinking that he would have charge of the pews up there, and asked a special favor of him: "Grant that these, my two sons, may sit the one on thy right hand and the other on thy left, in thy kingdom." She knew better than to ask for more than two sittings in that part of the house. She and Zebedee could "take

The Pew System

a turn about with the boys," she thought, and "there couldn't be any better place in the house." It was just such a location as she wanted.

The reply of the Lord was something like this: "Sittings are not mine to give. Pews are not sold in the kingdom of heaven. The Father will give you a seat if so be you are prepared, or enter in, desiring a place."

St. James understood the pew system when he instructed the ushers in his church as to their duties. "If there come into your assembly (or church) a man with a gold ring and goodly apparel, and there come in also a poor man in vile raiment; and ye have respect to him that weareth the gay clothing and say unto him, 'Sit thou here in a good place' (in the middle section with the four hundred) and say to the poor 'Stand thou there or sit here'(under the gallery) are ye not partial in yourselves and are become judges of evil thoughts?"

Many shall come from the east and from the west and shall sit down with Abraham, Isaac and Jacob. I shouldn't wonder if Mr. and Mrs. Brown and their whole family found room next to Abraham; and the Wymans, who left our church because they couldn't possibly pay for a seat (though they were offered one free under the gallery if they would stay) may sit next to the Patriarch Jacob, in the Church of the First Born.

CHAPTER VI

Parting Scenes

The parting day arrived. John, calm, earnest, entered the door with me and conducted me to my seat. It was his custom to go in at the people's door occasionally. It was one of John's peculiarities. He used to say that he got an inspiration from facing the pulpit, if only for a moment. He liked a genial smile from a friend in the vestibule or a warm shake of the hand as he passed down the aisle. There is sympathy in the air while one waits his turn at the duster by the outer door of a summer morning, and then grasps the handle of the wisp, warm from the touch of a friend.

As John passed up the steps to the platform, a sight met his eyes that was unexpected and made him hesitate to look. The whole house was filled with fruit. Grapes on their long vines draped the stained windows. Apples on their stout branches swayed from the pillars. Golden pumpkins, and pale bean vines, and great sheaves of wheat and rye loaded the platform. Corn, braided by its husks, still undried, was laid across the pulpit and trailed away down

Parting Scenes

the aisles. In front, suspended by an invisible wire, was the motto, "By their fruits ye shall know them."

John understood it all—this more than well-meant compliment to his labors. It had been done by a few that loved him and, now that he was actually going away, there was much of the love of the old times welling up from hearts that had suddenly remembered.

The human heart is so contrary with itself. We knew that there was sincere sorrow at a departure which had been forced by "unavoidable circumstances."

It is always a sad hour when a pastor says "farewell." There are the children over whose tiny forms he has bowed and murmured "In the Name of the Father," while as yet that Father's touch was warm upon them. There are the "mated pairs" upon whose union the hand of legal beatitude was laid by that same pastor. And there are those to whose homes came the most dreadful of all visitants, who were taught by this same pastor that hope is stronger than despair. Yes, a farewell sermon is sad.

John was equal to the occasion that day. He hesitated, changed color, glanced at the beautiful and generous display before him, and then with a slow sweep of his splendidly tearful eyes he looked every one of the great audience in the

Parting Scenes

face. There was not a word spoken by him, nor a rustle of sound among his people. There was the still pressing of handkerchiefs to flowing eyes, and then the whole congregation struck up the old hymn which, like ancient treasures of any sort, is rich because it has been kept so long—"When all thy mercies, O my God." As the "love and praise" of the last line died away, I began to dread the sermon. Farewell sermons are so sad; they make people cry over a minister whom they never saw before.

Now, I knew perfectly well that John would preach a good sermon. And I knew just as well, or thought I did, what it would be about.

I had never heard John preach a farewell sermon, but I had a great many others, and had become so familiar with their particular features that I believe I could have delivered one myself with perfect accuracy.

Usually John and I talked over the sermons beforehand; but that week I had been so busy packing and receiving calls that the sermon had been quite forgotten by me. Speaking of calls, I remember full well how the house was crowded all day and far into the evening. The neighbors did not come to help me, nor to do any thing in particular but to cry. And what they were crying about it would take a philosopher to tell. If they had spent some of their tears

Parting Scenes

over the delinquent debt of the church, and thus have shown their love for John; or if they had wept over the fact that John was not paid his dues, then I could have seen some good in their crying. But, now that we were going away, to come and sit and weep as if there were a coffin in the house; dropping in with no intention whatever of righting wrongs, looking woful and gloomy, detaining me when I was so busy, staring into vacancy or my trunks as occasion offered—all this set me to thinking. I didn't cry any, though my visitors did their best to persuade me.

Some, who wept most freely, I had scarcely ever known. Now I do cry myself, sometimes, but never before strangers if I can help it. John and I agree that if one makes the exhibition of emotion too common, feeling loses its effect. If one sheds tears profusely in the presence of strangers one naturally suspects affectation. A show of sorrow is sometimes extorted by the consideration of effect. In the case of my callers it was all for effect, save in a few instances when old friends broke down and my own eyes were reluctantly suffused.

John says there is an abnormal condition of the mind in some people, a chronic malady as it were, inducing its victim to seek opportunities for crying. Some crave sad emotion, as de-

Parting Scenes

ranged constitutions crave chalk and blue clay. They seek funerals, and death-beds, and convicts' cells, and revival meetings, and retiring ministers' families for the occasion thus obtained to enjoy their favorite occupation of shedding tears.

When John reads this he will say, "Aren't we uncharitable, dear? I am afraid you will hurt somebody's feelings; besides, you ought not to tell everybody what I say." And I will answer, "O John, I do not wish to offend anyone. I wish to write what is good and true and helpful. All these things happened a good while ago, you know, and may be they are out of fashion by this time. It may be impossible for the shoe I am cobbling to fit any modern foot. May be people will be interested to know what was the style in churches before they were born. I don't make up anything, you know; I write just what I can remember."

John will smile and say, "Well, my dear, be sure and write in the past tense, then. You forget and say 'are' for 'were' and 'is' for 'was.'"

I will try to remember, but if I forget occasionally, I beg to be excused.

As I said, I felt perfectly sure what the farewell sermon would be like. It would be the familiar one, of course—the text taken from Acts xx. There would be the venerable form of St.

Parting Scenes

Paul, and the roar of the sea, and the sobbing of the tide, and the tears alike of the people and of the briny deep. There would be the ship at anchor swaying in the blue, rocking to and fro from sympathy with the mourners on the shore. There would be the sea birds dropping their wings at half=mast, and dipping the tips of them in the surf as if to borrow tears. We should see St. Paul moving slowly down the beach, pausing where the white foam made no contrast with his hair as white. We should hear him deliver that never=to=be=forgotten farewell sermon that goes echoing down the ages with its own inimitable pathos. And there would come the prayer, when the voice was drowned in the depths, the words of which we shall never know till the day when the sea gives up its treasures.

Picture grand beyond description! Well was it painted on the shoreless sea whose outward horizon blended with the eternal sky! "And they accompanied him unto the ship," as far as any of us may accompany those we love. The white sails unfurl and we are left with the billows and our tears.

CHAPTER VII
John's Farewell Sermon

I am sure the congregation were all expecting that sermon, for they wept softly as if to be ready for the sorrowful climax. It was "as still as the grave," so to speak, when John arose and opened the Bible.

What was my surprise when he announced his text to be Genesis vi: 14.

How many thoughts crowd into the mind in a few seconds! They are like a vast throng of passers-by, not waiting for single file, but pushing and crowding themselves and jostling one another, without order or rank. I thought of the great disappointment depicted upon many faces; of John's lost opportunity of making a lasting impression; a personal impression; of his apparent lack of sympathy with the sad spirit of the hour, and of the criticism of those not in accord at any time. I knew the selection must be some account of the flood, and it seemed so unfitting. It was like a play announced to be "Love's drama," and when the curtain rose presenting only sea and sky.

But these feelings of mine were only for a mo-

John's Farewell Sermon

ment. My habitual confidence in John led me into serenity. It was so like John to choose the text he did. I remembered how I had heard him say that "ministers have no right to carry their personal feelings into their opportunities to preach. Personal love, sorrow, pique, fears, discontent, gratitude, have no place in the pulpit. When the preacher is done he will have led his hearers away from himself so that they will be conscious of nothing but the message. The hearers may think of themselves, and burn with sorrow, or pale with remorse; their sympathies may be aroused for some other, but not for the minister. *He should be in the background and preach Jesus Christ, not himself.*"

I think John was right. There is a great temptation for ministers to elicit sympathy for themselves, taking occasion from their privilege in the pulpit. Personal reminiscences of a private nature, allusions to great sorrows of their own which have no bearing upon the needs of the hour, have little effect save to cause tears to flow from eyes that are seldom dry. Intimations as to the depth of degradation into which they were plunged "before their conversion"; hints, with sighs as to possible "griefs" which they are keeping to themselves—all this is but vanity and vexation.

John's Farewell Sermon

These should be left in the study; abandoned with morning prayers. As to that farewell sermon enacted on the shores of the Mediterranean, there are few Pauls and as few opportunities to bid a last adieu to friends with breaking hearts. When "bonds and imprisonments" await the retiring minister; when he steps on shipboard to face a stronger and more cruel element than the sea, then may he appropriate to himself that matchless farewell. But to bring that sublime scene down to the conditions of to-day, when the retiring minister boards the train for an adjoining city, or steps out of one pulpit to take charge of another at more salary and less work, it is sacrilege. The conceit of it is appalling. And yet who stops to think?

There was a rustle visible and audible when John read: "Rooms shalt thou make in the ark, and thou shalt pitch it within and without with pitch."

"O John, John," I said to myself, "what can pitch possibly have to do with this church and with this occasion?" and I more than half smiled. I caught John's eye for an instant and in the flash was an assurance.

That habit of "catching John's eye" is a little custom, common to us even now that we are growing old and wear spectacles. That is what is meant by the text "As iron sharpeneth iron,

John's Farewell Sermon

so doth the countenance of a man his friend."

Mine is not the only eye that John used to catch. There was Judge Rich. John often says that Judge Rich, by a glance, has given him a new thought or checked him in some previously constructed utterance. He and the Judge, as well as John and I, sometimes made up the sermon together, or at least laid the foundation and put up the beams and rafters. Or we frescoed the whole when it was completed. John says this is what is meant by "the whole body fitly joined together." Every "joint" supplying what will be the most effectual "working" so that "love is edified." And "love was edified" that morning while the autumn sunshine streamed through the stained windows, giving the corn a purple tint and the wheat a crimson hue.

I wish I could give the sermon as a whole; but John's notes were abbreviated and even they are lost now. What I can remember of it I will give, however disconnected and insufficient. It may prove that the need of pitch is not lost even though the waters that bore Noah's ark are assuaged.

He first spoke of the need of an ark for individuals and for families. "What have you built," he asked "for the saving of your house? Everywhere is the flood of sin and the debris of

John's Farewell Sermon

misery cast up by sin. The driftwood of crime, committed or intended, seeks a shore upon which to cast itself. What about the church, this ark that you are in? Have you pitched it within and without with pitch? Have you sealed the apertures through which vainglory, and presumption, and unsanctified ambition, and envy and strife seep and filter? Have you made the roof secure, that part next to God and heaven, over which Justice bends and Eternity holds its possibilities?

"Perchance you have pitched it 'without.' To the world, which sees only the exterior, you are safe. The rains descend and the floods come; you shelter yourselves behind the walls that enclose you. You do a thousand things under cover of the ark, under the wings of the church, assuring yourselves that there is no danger. Are there not envy, and overreaching, and backbiting, and discontent, and deception? Is there not the slander of a look, the stain of a half-uttered exclamation? Are there not bargains and sales in which the consideration is a mortgage on the soul and values paid in gold coined from life's best possibilties? Is there not the preferring of a man's self to his neighbor, the scuffle of hurrying feet to secure the best things, the best homes and the best privileges?

John's Farewell Sermon

"Listen!" and there was perfect silence for minutes. Then John went on: "Do you hear all these, oozing drop by drop, through your ark? Oh, the empty profession; the lack of pitch on the inside; the forgetting of possible crevices out of sight of scrutiny; the neglect of invisible apertures through which the storm drizzles!

"The story of the flood has not lost its meaning. The command of Jehovah, 'Thou shalt pitch it within and without with pitch,' was not given to be spent upon a structure three hundred cubits long and thirty cubits high. The character of a man stretches from life's bit of shore into the surge of eternity. It may be as high as it is long and reach to the sky above him. A man's character is his ark. In his heart, in the inside of him, he must be impervious to the elements. If this inside be neglected, the outside, his pretension, his common life, is full of chinks. Through these the flood sweeps, and the agitated outer elements surge.

"Men may build an ark whose form is good. They may make for themselves 'rooms' wherein to house the creatures of Christian culture. But if it be not cemented together part to part, of what avail?

"Varnish is not cement. In a little space of time a man will be as if he had no ark. And the worst of it is, when a man's ark is sub-

John's Farewell Sermon

merged, from whatever disaster, his household mostly perish with him. Is your life consistent, my hearers? Have you constructed your ark, be it church, or home, or character, with an eye to the danger? Beware of the little leaks, the seams, the fissures, through which the floods that are without may reach you."

And then John spoke of the "ark of bullrushes" in which a royal infant was placed upon the river. How it, too, "was daubed with pitch," that it should not sink with the weight of its occupant. "Happy the man," he said, "whose ark is built in childhood. Save a child and perchance you save a prophet. See to it that no chink is left in the little bark through which may gurgle the rush of high water or the ooze of low tide."

And then he turned the Bible over and on until he reached the Revelation.

"And I saw a new heaven and a new earth, for the first heaven and the first earth had passed away, and there was no more sea." The flood has spent itself. The first heaven, with its clouds and booming storms and rushing mighty winds has passed away. So has the first earth, on whose bosom were agitation and the moan of waves and the ceaseless roar of unrest.

"What is your prospect, my hearers, as you look out of your windows? To some of you the

John's Farewell Sermon

tops of the mountains above the clouds are already visible. Ararat is in sight. Yet seven days, mayhap, and your ark will rest upon the summit. See, the rainbow, God's promise, spans the arch of time's horizon. Though the flood is not yet subsided there is the bow. 'And there shall be no more sea.' 'No more sea'."

John himself was forgotten. It was as he would have it. There was a hush of many minutes when it seemed as if we heard the swish of waters, and the gentle dying away of rain, and the low grinding of the boat's bottom on the sand, while tints of rainbow colors fell softly through the windows. We saw the new heaven and the new earth. St. John, sitting alone on the Isle of Patmos, faded into a distant speck and then sank into a blending of earth and sky radiant with light.

Then the choir sang that hymn of Faber's. Low and soft the melody approached us from far away. Nearer it came, and then it receded until we could only hear a faint tone as of distant waves at daybreak:

> The land beyond the sea;
> When will life's task be o'er?
> When shall we reach that soft blue shore,
> O'er the dark strait whose billows foam and roar?
> When shall we come to thee,
> Calm land beyond the sea?

CHAPTER VIII

John Finds a New Field

After we bade good-by to the church that outgrew John we went into the country where we owned a little cottage and some acres. John was urged to take another charge immediately, but he declined, saying that "he would wait a while."

John did not claim the need of "rest," that excuse for all the follies and embarrassments and illnesses that ministerial flesh is heir to. He says: "Ministers do not need rest more than two-thirds of the flock need it. It is change, not rest, which they all need. It would be better for both the preacher and his people if the minister took a turn about with the husbandman and the house-builder and the teacher. They would all secure the needed change, and the pulpit might not suffer if the gospel were presented now and then from the standpoint of a lay member. The fact is, the minister grows naturally into viewing all sides of faith and practice from the observatory of the pulpit, hence he is so often shocked at what he terms heterodoxy in some of his flock. Meanwhile the

John Finds a New Field

member wonders that his spiritual leader is so near-sighted.

"What the preacher needs occasionally is steady work for muscles of chest and hand and limb a part of every year. There would be fewer cases of 'nervous prostration' sent across the seas to recuperate, and less sentiment about 'wearing oneself out in the service.' Martyrs in this sense are not needed. When a minister begins to look pale and pathetic, and bends his head languidly to one side in a pensive way, and elicits sympathy on account of his 'nerves,' it is high time the church door were closed on him and he, like Adam, sent into the garden to dress and to keep it. This would not be degrading to the ministry, but uplifting. Such a course would ensure a return to the pulpit with new thoughts and finer perceptions caught from plants and animals and fresh air. The 'Tree of Life' grows in the garden to-day no less than it did in Adam's day; and we die with our years half told for want of the thing, which by reason of its very nearness, we neglect. Away with the pensive cast of countenance too often seen in the pulpit! Let it give willing place to temporary sunburn. Callous hands may point the way to heaven as accurately as softly dimpled ones."

That is what John says, and I answer: "Don't you think you are too severe yourself this time?

John Finds a New Field

You might give offense, you know, to real good ministers. Ministers are spiritual folks; why, I know of one who was dismissed from a very fine situation because he was seen, in broad daylight, carrying a piece of stovepipe home under his arm. And another was criticised sharply for being seen with a pair of old trousers on, digging in the garden around some shrubs. I tell you, John, ministers can't be too careful."

"No, ministers can't be too careful," echoed John. "I have heard too many allusions to a certain minister's 'faultless complexion,' or to his small and shapely hands. The elegance of his person too often decides in favor of a new pastor. Not that grace of figure nor of feature are to be disparaged. They are gifts of God—but there are other gifts."

John tilled his acres for a year and then he taught school a term. Those are old-fashioned methods of change and recuperation viewed from the height of the present time. Even at the date of my story wise old heads could be seen shaking wofully and hinting at "time wasted" and "talents buried in a napkin."

John made answer: "It was not that the talent was wrapped in a napkin, but that it was buried, that brought censure upon the servant. It was put out of sight, out of mind, out of touch, out of circulation in a world of traffic

John Finds a New Field

which had need of it. The napkin was but a girdle, or the wallet in which the talent should have been carried about with the servant. My talent, the silver negotiable in the kingdom, is in the wallet of my faith. I shall not bury it in my field, albeit I am ploughing and planting. The Lord's money is no less at interest that I myself am the usurer. It is accumulating to itself more of its kind, and the whole sum is ready at the call of the Master."

Thus did John make answer in regard to his so-called buried talent. All the time he was thinking and reading—"whetting his scythe," as he said. At the end of two years he was ready for a new swath. This was no sooner known than many were his invitations. He went about some and in a short time had decided in his own mind what field he would prefer. John had preferences. All ministers have.

He says: "It might be well for the minister to give the church a call, occasionally. Satisfaction would result as often, perhaps, and neither should make haste in the matter. One swallow does not make a summer, neither does one sermon nor even two prove the fitness of pastor to people. How can a preacher conclude that he is the man for a certain church when he knows nothing of that church save as he has looked upon a sea of faces? It has been re-

John Finds a New Field

ferred to on the part of his friends as 'a desirable field.' What constitutes a desirable field? Large numbers, fine equipments, generous salary?"

John did not choose "a desirable field." If so, then he would have accepted the invitation to Old Mentone, where he was offered five thousand and an assistant besides. "Just out of debt; large, fine church; good standing; high-toned; in fact, a model."

"And why should not we go there?" I asked. "You deserve it, John. You can grace any pulpit, and they want you. Besides, you have served your term with poverty and church debt and uncomfortable things." Oh, I did want to go to Old Mentone! John could do as much good there as elsewhere, I argued; and the church being so "united" upon giving him a "call" was the strongest reason why he should go there. In fact, it was an absolute "indication," and I told him so.

John found me crying one time about that very thing, for women will cry, even ministers' wives, sometimes. I had begun to suspect what his choice would be. When he saw my tears John took my hand and said, kindly: "There is the story of a woman who did wash the feet of the Christ with tears and wiped them with the hair of her head. It was not the fact that she

John Finds a New Field

wept that startled dignity—the greatest of them had no doubt wept. They would make haste to mingle their tears with the Great Master's, to baptize His hands or His forehead in the accepted dignity of tears. But to kneel at His feet, to wash *them*, to weep in a humiliating attitude, to choose a menial service while the multitudes were at meat—this is what shocked propriety, but it sent its holy lesson into all the world.

"There are many to sit at meat in the grand churches; there is no difficulty in filling the pulpits of such with eloquence. Will you come with me to this unfortunate church, so long relegated to fast on account of its sins, and there wash the Master's feet? In that place you could break the alabaster box of your heart with its hopes and desires and preferences, and even its love of me. The perfume of it all might fill the house and you yourself be charged with sweetness as you never would have been without the breaking of the box. What shall we do?"

When John said, "What shall we do?" his tone implied, "This thing will we do," and I knew he was right.

Now, the church that John chose was a very unpopular one, to say the best of it. His connection with it could not possibly bring him precedence nor honor. It had passed through

John Finds a New Field

one of those dire calamities of public scandal which spares neither pulpit nor pew. The church body itself was now nearly disbanded. Member after member had slipped out into other folds, or had retired altogether from Christian society. Its very name was a reproach to religion.

There was no church edifice, so to speak, but simply a plain two-story structure, much too large, without spire or bell or debt or other incumbrance save that dreadful scandal. For some time it had been difficult to supply the pulpit two Sundays in succession. A minister had no reward for preaching in that church outside of the very few dollars in his pocket. It gave him no popularity with other churches.

The membership which remained was divided into factions. There were backbitings and strife and evil surmisings. Upon one thing only were they all agreed—they must have a pastor or disband altogether.

In speaking of our going there John said to me: "There was a certain man going down from Jerusalem to Jericho who fell among thieves. These stripped him of his raiment and wounded him and departed, leaving him half dead. We have found this church, this 'certain man'; shall we pass him by like the characters in the story, or shall we tarry and have compassion and bind

John Finds a New Field

up his wounds and take care of him; seat him on our own beast, figuratively speaking—that principle, or power, or divine means of overcoming the roughness of the way by which we ourselves have journeyed so far? This church has been sick a long while. It has little strength and less courage to use what strength it has. It imagines every man a robber and is afraid to move lest it meet again with calamity.

"Jesus stood up in the synagogue and read about healing the broken-hearted, delivering the captives, preaching the acceptable year of the Lord, giving sight to the blind and taking care of them that are bruised. Who is broken-hearted more than the church that has endured such a scandal? Who is a captive more than this church chained to the dead body of a criminal—the memory of such a shame? The members are cast down, evilly spoken of, full of bitterness and reproach for one another, and hate and evil thoughts. It has not a single attractive feature save its scars."

I do not mean my description shall be absolutely sweeping. There were a few men and women who bore up under the derision and deserved scorn, whose own skirts were free from pollution save as they had suffered from bearing the common burden.

How sin hardens the human heart! I do

John Finds a New Field

mean more the hearts of those who have sinned primarily, than I do friends and observers. From being at first distressed, and humiliated, and grieved, they soon grow morose and unforgiving. This was the case with that church at Sunrise Park.

CHAPTER IX

At Sunrise Park

There was enough support pledged to John to keep us from anxiety. He would accept of no promises beyond their present ability. We could live comfortably and save a little. This was as well as the majority of members did. "The workman is worthy of his meat," John quoted. "It is not necessary that he dine on terrapin and robins' breasts. He may share the meat of those about him, be it only bacon and mutton brisket, provided those about him can no afford better, and over it say 'grace' for the whole community."

As I said, we had sufficient and some to spare for an occasional tramp. By "tramp" I mean a visitor of whatsoever sort. What else do we mean when we pray, "Give us this day our daily bread?" The personal pronoun "I" is not used in the Lord's Prayer, hence we pray for the tramp—the disagreeable, homespun tramp—who comes to us unannounced and uninvited, save as we invited him unconsciously in our petition.

John says: "There are tramps, and other

At Sunrise Park

tramps. Some go about on foot in threadbare clothes, and countenances as threadbare of hope or of shame. These are the unwelcome, hated tramps, who steal a night's lodging on our hay and sneak away in the early dawn. They are as shiftless and as lazy as was that class mentioned in the Levitical law, who no doubt objected to hard work, but who nevertheless were provided for. 'Thou shalt not glean thy vineyard, neither shalt thou gather every grape of thy vineyard; thou shalt leave them for the poor and stranger (the tramps); I am the Lord *your* God.'

"There are some who tramp in private cars fitted into moving palaces, who dine at grand hotels, instead of on our back door-steps. These also we include in the prayer for 'our daily bread.' The 'family and fold of God' include all classes. Conditions are accepted with a sigh in the present state of society. When the vineyards revert to the original owner, Jehovah, there will be no grudging of the gleanings for the poor. And Jehovah respects toil and ownership, for the tramp was not entitled to the first harvest. A handful of barley, a small share only of the abundant whole, was left for the stranger. He had no right to another man's labor. This system kept the one from starving, while the other was taught to remember the poor."

At Sunrise Park

We moved into a small cottage in the rural village of Sunrise Park in June 18—. John's first sermon was on the text, "As long as the cloud abode upon the tabernacle they rested in their tents." "God would teach his people to rest when the cloud is on them, when the mists of reproach and trial are between them and light. To rest was to feel no doubt in the ultimate moving on; to feel secure and at home with God's promises even though one's way lay through the wilderness. Jehovah is not the cloud, but He is in the cloud. We bless His holy name for that. Though there seems no light in your way, and each has been separated from his brother on account of the thick darkness, there are promises to you like light to the blind. Here is one: 'As a shepherd seeketh out his flock in the day that he is among his sheep that are scattered, so will I seek out my sheep and will deliver them out of all places where they have been scattered in the cloudy and dark day.' Ye are all the Lord's Israel, and the promises are unto you and to your children."

And "rest" fell upon the handful of believers in the little troubled church. New tissue began to form in the bruised places; old torn shreds began to knit to the better structures, and although the processes were slow they were healthy.

At Sunrise Park

I say the work of repair "began"; there was no miracle wrought in an hour. Natural growth out of trouble was simply fostered and perfected by grace. "First that which is natural" came about. Time heals, to some extent, spiritual as well as physical wounds. Natural processes do their healing work in body and in heart. They are none the less of God.

If I were writing an impossible story I would have that unfortunate church brought into unity and sweetness of temper and love unfeigned in the twinkling of an eye. That would illustrate the power of John's influence and put him on the plane of the old prophets who caused iron to swim and leprosy to disappear in a river bath. But John was not one of the old prophets, and as this is a true story I cannot record flattering results.

There were no swift changes for the better; no success on lightning wings as a reward for self-abandonment. Some great and unexpected good comes to the boy in the Sunday-school book and he tantalizes his companions who are not good, with a display of his gain.

It is only a story conceived by the author to induce all little boys to be good. There is not a particle of truth in it. The result is, if a boy is good and obedient and the reward is not forthcoming he pouts and grows sullen. A bit

At Sunrise Park

of Sunday-school fiction has spoiled many a boy. Better to have taught the lesson that visible reward is as scarce as humming birds at Christmas time when the snow is three feet deep in the garden. Reward is not more sure to the boy than is success to the man. Both may come in disguise and never be recognized in this life.

So, as I said, results in John's work were not soon nor flattering. The command to "wash and be clean" was to individuals, not communities. One at a time the maimed, the lame, the halt and the blind go down into the pool, angel-troubled. It is heaven's method of receiving the sick. One at a time is healed of whatsoever disease he has. If the healing were to reach all at once, where were patience, and the watching for repeated visits of the angel, and the great desire to step down first? When, by a manifold miracle ten were cleansed, only one returned to give glory. Glory is necessary to convince the world, and so we have one leper at a time cleansed.

In this new field of his John did not expect immediate and universal results. "Hadst thou faith like a grain of mustard seed thou couldst say to this mountain, 'Be thou removed,' and it would obey thee." "Like a grain of mustard seed" perfect, fertile, without suspicion of for-

At Sunrise Park

eign element or premature putting forth—a thing measured and weighed and fashioned according to some mysterious power. Faith like a grain of mustard seed is not common, even if it be found at all in the church of God. Some are said to possess it, but who has removed a mountain? To level a tiny hillock is easy, but where whole mountains of accumulated misery stretch across the church continent there are none with faith like a mustard seed to command them to be removed. A mountain is seen of many; it is not a *mound* on one's personal estate whose exact location and size none may know save the owner of it. I may claim to have removed a mountain in my pasture lands, but unless it has been located and measured and scaled by others besides myself, who shall believe that I have removed a mountain? Nor were we commanded to remove mountains.

CHAPTER X

A Church Reception

Soon after our arrival at Sunrise Park the church gave a reception to the new pastor. Church receptions in those days days were often peculiar. The "leading members"—that is, the smart, well dressed, fine, fashionable minority of the real whole—constituted themselves a "reception committee." They gathered in a circle in the centre of the church parlor, smiling and chatting and diffusive of witty remarks. When the new minister and his wife appeared they were introduced to the waiting ring in succession, and afterwards, poor, insignificant members were hurriedly or carelessly presented. Naturally enough, and without evident intention, these were passed along to make room for others. The affectionate "leading members" managed always to have the minister in charge, very much as its owners guard a beautiful animal at a county fair. He is dextrously engaged in conversation by the brightest ladies, and occasionally with some gentleman of the same sort. So adroitly is the event managed that at the close of the affair the minister imag-

A Church Reception

ines that his flock are all South Downs without a mixture of inferior stock, and he wonders that "the lines have fallen to him in such pleasant places." Alas for the church of God if "pleasant places" are the ambition of her ministers! —unless, perchance, their ambition be to make "pleasant places" for those of the flock who are on the remote desert edge of poverty and unpopularity.

There! I am guilty of a solecism—the very thing John bade me beware of. I dropped from the past to the present tense. It was unintentional; of course I was describing a church reception as it *was*, not as it *is*.

It was a bright picture that met us at the door. Being in perfect health at the time and in the best of spirits, John and I were prepared to enjoy the reception. We were presented to "the committee," and afterwards to each and all in turn. Then seats were placed for us against a background of flowers and vines.

I whispered to John a suggestion that we were in danger of being carried to the skies "on flowery beds of ease," but he bade me have no fear.

Pots of rare fragrance were set all about on little tables so that the whole air was redolent. Pretty dresses and shining white teeth and brilliant conversation made me, at least, very

A Church Reception

happy and flattered; nor was I proof against the pleasant personal things said to me. I did my best to return in kind all that I received, inwardly assured that in such polite and finished society I should have nothing to regret. Alas, and alas!

Soon John began to look uninterested. Once or twice he did not hear when a remark was made to him. I understood. Some thoughtless people were "bringing up a slander on the land," and John did not care to hear. Small-talk like this was repulsive to him as in bad taste in such a place, aside from its bearing upon his connection with every separate member of his flock.

He turned and looked around the large room. I followed his glance and saw what I had not noticed before—that we were the centre of a group of the best dressed, most aristocratic people in the parlor. To the left of us there was a second group—second in appearance, though not lacking in a certain refinement one sees in some who wear second-rate clothes. In the far corner was yet another group, of the more common sort who work diligently, live economically and pay their debts; at the same time wearing their last year's bonnets and coats with a certain "at-homeness" quite possible with such out-of-date apparel. One sees this identical

CONVERSING AWHILE WITH HIS NEW CONSTITUENCY.

A Church Reception

group in some of the churches of to-day, I am told. They pay their church dues promptly and are never behind in their obligations, whether sacred or secular. And yet, strange to say, they are always in the "far corner." They are treated respectfully, to be sure; even cordially when there is an especial collection to be taken. In the intervals they are always to be found in that "far corner." I wish there were no corners in the church; no distance suggestive of groups.

John excused himself and walked over to group No. 2. I could see speaking glances dart from one to another of the little faction about me and there was quite a hush in the hitherto lively conversation. After conversing a while with his new constituency, John went over to the far corner. I could see, by his manner, and the way in which he was drawing everyone into conversation, that he was very much interested there. Presently he called to someone in group No. 2 to come over into the corner and decide some question. This made a break in group No. 2, and soon the whole of them were in the corner. But it seemed the question under discussion could not be settled without group No. 1 joined the combine. It was appealed to, and of course we, too, went over into the corner. John was always a good talker. By "good talker" I do not mean that he said so

A Church Reception

much himself, though he was not lacking in expression, but he had a gift of making others give an opinion or venture a remark, which was irresistible.

The subject of conversation that evening was "Individuality in plants and animals," of course including man. The personality of every separate apple blossom and its apparent determination to develop itself into an apple; the impression it makes upon a neighboring apple by close association, as is noticed in the light and shade of coloring. There is a like personality in vegetables which crowd together in the ground. The stronger shape the weaker and crush them into dwarfs—misshapen semblances of the vegetables they ought to be. Only to beings of human growth has been given the divine behest to "look also upon the things of others," or to "prefer one another in honor" or perfectness. If the "Son of man should walk through the fields on the Sabbath day" as he did so long ago, would he not find his people, like the lower orders, crowding one another, and crushing the small ones, and pushing each in turn, or all the time, his fellows, until the nourishment intended for the whole is absorbed by a few, and the little ones left to wither?

"But don't you think," said a lady in gray, "that the little ones ought to be glad to see the

A Church Reception

big ones grow and be beautiful? And after all, do not the small ones push just as hard to get to the light and crowd themselves between better individuals—as, see the apples in a cluster? They started together in the blossom. Whose fault is it that one is full-grown and the other dwarfed?"

"First that which is natural," replied John, "and afterwards that which is spiritual. The Son of man came to teach that individuality should give place to preference, and personal ambition for place or prominence to stand aside for the good of all. Though like them in many ways, are we not much better than the plants?"

"Well," said a gentleman with a dress-coat on, "I fail to see the point in all this. The sentiment is good but where shall we apply it? If a man is never to rise unless he lift his neighbor with him, how many of us would be above the turf? I am on the south side of the apple tree, just where nature hung me. Shall I leave my place and swing around to the north that my little neighbor in the shade may have the light? Or, I am a potato in the garden soil. Am I to squeeze under a smaller one, between it and some other, that they may have more room to grow on the outside and suck in the moisture of the surface where I had my birthright? Sir, it is unnatural. Ten to one the

A Church Reception

little one would never grow to my size if it had a chance."

Here a call to supper interrupted the conversation and the subject was postponed to the next social. It was a good deal better to carry on a conversation in this way on various subjects than to stand or sit, looking tired or parading one's clothes or dividing into groups for gossip.

One of the gentlemen beside me gave me his arm and I heard him suggest to a neighbor that he arrange for the minister to take Mrs. McDeavitt. "A highly respectable lady," as he whispered to me.

I looked at Mrs. McDeavitt and noted her beauty, her faultless dress and manner—but alas! there was about her a certain undefinable air which bade me beware. Immediately upon the proposal for tea I saw John give his arm to a diffident, plainly dressed woman by his side, a Miss Waterbury.

Again the reception committee exchanged glances. But I was glad for John, and glad for the lady by his side as well. I thought she looked as if she would grace a better station in life than she was used to. That was a very foolish thought of mine; as if any position were not "graced" by such as she. When shall we learn that there is no station better than the one that

A Church Reception

each is in, provided each graces that position?

Of course, way was made for the minister and his companion to pass out ahead, and he seated her with the deference so natural to John. She looked happy, as if conscious of having swung around "to the south side of the apple tree," and she grew rosy in the sunshine of her new place.

I looked down the table and noted that the "sets" or factions were seated as they had stood before—in separate companies. There was no mingling of either with the other, save in the case of Rachel Waterbury. And yet this was at the Lord's table, and in His house!

CHAPTER XI

We Receive Calls

The church social was a success in that his people began to understand John on the "church-gossip" question. Some people think there is a sacredness about church gossip which naturally places it above the ordinary, and lends it an air of tolerance quite foreign to common smalltalk. But John says "church gossip has no more sanctity than neighborhood slander; in fact it is more malicious." What should the new minister care that this or that member "was concerned in the late trouble and took sides" one way or another?

Some sly attempts were made afterwards to interest John and me in the past painful history of the church, but I do not know to this day who was to blame and who not in the matter, nor the particulars as to the slander.

The past was forgotten save as we could see the "cold shoulder" on the part of some of the flock towards other members.

There was a disposition to be "neighborly" on the part of some of our neighbors, especially those who lived close by. Such as did not

We Receive Calls

"drop in" just to get acquainted with the new minister and see "how he stood" on the questions of the day, came in to get acquainted with the minister's wife. They came at all hours and stayed until they had to go home to get dinner or supper, or put the children to bed. Sometimes a well=meaning woman came before breakfast and stopped for half an hour. But the favorite time seemed to be about the middle of the forenoon; just when I was the busiest. I took it all in good part, thinking it one of the duties of a minister's wife to be agreeable and make others happy.

At first my neighbors rang the front door bell, as neighbors should; then they took to knocking at the back door, and finally they walked directly in, saying, as the door opened without warning, "Its just me," or "Now, don't get up."

Almost all housekeepers like privacy, and I do most heartily. When it comes to community of homes I am decidedly conservative. So is John. So was St. Paul when he enjoined women to "be discreet, chaste keepers at home." Whose home did he mean, their own or their neighbor's home?

Now we are social, John and I. We like company at the proper time. But the disorderly running out and in of neighbors, the presuming upon a friend's courtesy, the idle, mo-

We Receive Calls

tiveless calling that unemployed women so often do, is not uplifting. One does not like to be caught cleaning out the stove with a towel pinned about one's head, nor brushing down the dressers, nor dusting the parlor. In spite of native politeness or acquired courtesy there is an inward distress at such moments, and an unexpressed wish that one's friends "would call in the afternoon."

I tried to be sweet-tempered and cordial to my neighbors, even though their calling caused delay in a hundred things, in spite of their oft-repeated injunctions to "go right on now just as if we wasn't here." I reasoned that these were the customs of the village; besides I realized that there is a sort of possession of the minister and his whole family by all the flock, or the flock take it for granted.

John suggested that an easy way out of the trouble would be for me to "have a day." So I wrote "Mondays" on the lower left-hand corner of my visiting cards and believed it would work. But it did not. Some came on Monday, but the majority declared they wouldn't go to see any woman "on her day." They "came to see me," and they wanted to "catch me just as I was." I needn't have a day on their account; they "could come any time."

They blindly refused to see that it was for my

We Receive Calls

own convenience that I had "a day." Some of my friends affected to take offense, declaring that I was "putting on airs" and "trying to be like city folk" in having a day on my card.

I could have got along with all this well enough with my usual foolish excuse that I was "helping John," but when it came to *borrowing*, I needed a great deal of "grace" to overcome my natural feelings. I had to think about "John's work" a good deal before I was resigned; but when I once gave up on this point I did it heartily. John and I make it a rule to borrow nothing. If we desire something which is not at hand, we go without or wait till we can buy it. This as a rule. But these people to whom we had come as strangers seemed to consider us and our belongings as their own. There was no time, no household stuff, no personal strength, which was ours positively.

I do not think they intended to impose upon us in any way. I am sure they did not. They were simply uneducated in these points, as I have since learned is the case with many admirable people. Like many another minister's flock, they simply presumed upon the minister's good nature in a thoughtless sort of way. Did he not belong to them? Did they not pay him a salary?—hence he and his wife and all their personal effects were theirs.

We Receive Calls

"Mother wants to know if she can borrow some of the morning's milk; she'll pay it back to-night." Or "Mother wants to borrow your cutting shears." Or "Aunt Jane says, 'Will you loan her some tea and a pan of flour?'" These are samples of the requests that came in at the kitchen door. Many a time have I loaned my thick shawl or my best gloves or even John's overcoat to parties going for a drive; and to the same parties many times over. Thread, spoons, books, the children's playthings, chairs, and garden hose, each and all played their part in this neighborly kindness. Most of the things were returned in good shape, though invariably they were retained for a longer time than had been expected, and sometimes I was obliged to send for them. Often, I am sorry to say, in the matter of butter, tea, flour, etc., inferior articles were sent home to me.

This went on for a while and then our neighbors came to borrowing *me.* Was anybody sick in the village the minister's wife was sent for. She was expected to leave her babies with the minister, her dough in the pan, her dusting half done, her new book half read, her letters unfinished. She must sit up with the dying, lay out the dead babies, stay with the family in their hour of affliction, assist at births and funerals, superintend the wedding cake and the bride's

MOTHER WANTS TO BORROW SOME OF THE MORNING'S MILK.

We Receive Calls

trousseau; in short, the minister's wife was "maid-of-all-work" in the church.

I would not mention all this if I did not know that many a minister's wife has had a like experience; on a smaller scale, mayhap, but little less realistic.

I never complained; I took it for granted in some vague way that I was "helping John in his work" to thus become a martyr. And yet in what particular way all this was helping him I never stopped to conjecture. In some mystical way I was "bearing my cross." I "ought to be glad of doing some good in the world" I argued, while I thought of my neglected duties. "A minister's wife has a great responsibility."

Yes, a great responsibility. In my case I was responsible for the selfishness of my neighbors. I was humoring their greed and covetousness. I was myself unconsciously aiding them in breaking the decalogue. I was robbing my family of what they were entitled to—my best self. I kept these things to myself as far as was possible, not wishing to bother John, naturally, as he had troubles of his own which I shall mention another time. But when it came to my being absent from home three days in the week and called up at midnight or at early dawn, of course John began to look up the matter.

CHAPTER XII

I Begin to Look Like a Minister's Wife

I was looking worn and haggard, thin in flesh and generally "run down" as the saying is. I noticed my forlorn appearance in the glass when I brushed my hair that was catching its premature sprinkling of gray. I felt even worse than I looked, so languid and weak, while ghostly shades of "nervous prostration" gave me the nightmare. I argued to myself: "That's the way ministers' wives all look. It's right, I suppose, that they should be worn out and grow old, young. They have a mission, a field of labor, and they ought not to think of themselves at all: that would be selfish and hinder their husbands' ministry."

One day John came in and found me getting ready to go away with a neighbor who was waiting in his carriage.

"Where are you going?" asked John.

"Why," I answered, "Mrs. Pliable's* little

*I have borrowed the names for this chapter from "Pilgrim's Progress" to avoid saying Mrs. Smith or Mrs. Jones too often. They will answer my purpose just as well.

I Look Like a Minister's Wife

Paul is very sick, indeed. The doctor says if he lives at all it will be by the very best of nursing, so they want me to come right over. I'll be back in time for supper if I can, though I suppose they'll want me to stay all night. I shall take the baby with me."

"My dear," said John, "lay off your bonnet; I will excuse you to Mr. Pliable," and he went out to the gate. I could see the two gentlemen from where I stood and also hear a part of their conversation.

"My wife is not looking well," John said to our neighbor. "Will you kindly excuse her to Mrs. Pliable and say that we hope the best for the child?"

"But," pleaded Mr. Pliable, "my wife is nearly worn out and must have help. There is not a nurse to be had for less than ten dollars a week and they are scarce at that price. Our former minister's wife always stayed with the sick and afflicted."

"I am sorry," replied John, "but it is impossible."

Mr. Pliable rode away looking as if he had met with sudden reverses, while John came back to my room.

"You have acted as professional nurse for the last time," he said. "You have lost your bloom

I Look Like a Minister's Wife

and your step is heavy and slow. The children look unhappy and forlorn, as if they had lost their mother. As for myself I must have been asleep. I was busy and abstracted, inexcusably so, or I would have seen how things were going. Now put on your bonnet again and take a drive with me."

I did so most gladly; I had not taken a drive with John for a month. The breeze was invigorating and the sense of somebody coming between me and my deformed sense of duty was most refreshing. Still I felt a trifle ill at ease, for little Paul might die in the night and I be needed. My conscience, so long used to being gauged by the demands of others, reproached me, and I ventured to say to John: "I might have gone for to-day. I don't like to offend those good people, nor to be a drawback to you in your work. I want to be your helpmeet and I am afraid this sudden refusal will be an injury to you, dear."

"An injury to me!" John echoed, and he laughed heartily. "I had no intention of bringing my wife here to be a nurse and undertaker and maid-of-all-work for people in well-to-do circumstances who have no more conception of what is right and just than to ask you to do all this. Even if you were thoughtless enough to offer to do it they should not accept. I wonder

I Look Like a Minister's Wife

whence sprang the idea that a minister's wife is the perquisite of his flock, and who was responsible for the first female martyr in this line?"

"I don't know," I said, suddenly bereft of what I had considered good and sufficient reasons in time past. "Perhaps it was the custom of the early church. You know we are constantly finding out new things that the early church did. Paul said 'help those women who labored with us.' I suppose they had worn themselves out in helping take care of the sick and doing good generally. But aside from the early church, John, it must have been the original intention when Eve was created for a 'help=meet' for her husband."

"You emphasize the wrong word," John replied. "You should say help=*meet*, not *help*=meet. People mostly, even women themselves, italicise the *help* and so they go on doing what they have no right nor calling to do. Eve was to be a helpmeet for Adam, not a helpmeet for the whole thoughtless neighborhood. How can you be a help to me when you are tired and worn with other people's affairs? A minister's wife has as much right to personality as any other woman, and more. Where is my overcoat? The wind changes." "Oh," I said, "Mrs. By=ends borrowed it last week. Her husband was going to the beach and his coat was not ex-

I Look Like a Minister's Wife

actly the right weight, but they promised to bring it back in a week or two. I had forgotten all about it."

"I suppose," said John, "that the Feeble=minds have your warm shawl, and the Dare=not=lies your bread pans, and the Ready=to=halts your baby carriage. We will see about this."

When we got home John came in and took an inventory of household stock. It was as he had surmised. Almost every other thing in the kitchen department was loaned and a good deal of the clothing besides.

"This will never do," John said.

"Why, John!" I exclaimed, very much surprised, "does it not say in the Sermon on the Mount, 'Give to him that asketh of thee and from him that would borrow of thee turn not thou away?' And again, 'If any man sue thee at the law and take away thy coat give him thy cloak also?' How could I be obedient to this plain scripture=teaching if I refused to loan anything or even to give away if I were asked? We are to give everything asked of us. The words are plain and cannot mean anything else than what they say. Here is the Bible. Read it and see."

John read at the place I had turned to. "If any man will sue thee at the law and take away thy coat let him have thy cloak also," and

I Look Like a Minister's Wife

"Give to him that asketh of thee and from him that would borrow of thee turn not thou away." I felt sure that I had quoted the texts correctly and I was glad for John to see that I had acted conscientiously in the matter.

"Now," said John, "let us study this point and see how it stands. Jesus was bringing up some items in the old law. These could not but be familiar to the disciples. We will turn to Deut. xv. 8, 11. It is a command that we be pitiful to the poor and needy. 'Thou shalt not harden thy heart nor shut thy hand from thy poor brother, but thou shalt open thy hand wide unto him, and thou shalt surely lend him sufficient for his need in that which he wanteth. For the poor shall never cease out of the land, therefore I command thee saying thou shalt open thy hand wide unto thy brother, to thy poor, and to thy needy in thy land.'

"Now let us turn to Luke, sixth chapter, where the Master explains his meaning: 'If ye lend to them of whom ye hope to receive, what thank have ye?—for sinners also lend to sinners, to receive as much again. But love ye your enemies and do good, and lend hoping for nothing again.'

"There seem but two classes to whom it is our duty to lend,—the poor and our enemies. Our enemies are not likely to ask for a loan, and as for the other class, 'He that giveth to the

I Look Like a Minister's Wife

poor lendeth to the Lord.' If one whom we know to be our enemy were in need we might win him by the offer of a loan. He will not ask the favor. It is we who must make the advance."

"As to giving one's coat away there is good ground for that, under conditions. If a man sue thee at the law, if thou hast wronged any man to so great an extent that he may have recourse to the law, and so the justice of his complaint is made clear, give him more than restitution. Double the sum which was his by right, thereby confessing thy own sin and making it possible for you to love each other as you never could if thou hadst not given thy cloak also. It is impossible for two parties to meet on this ground and maintain the old resentment. How many have had recourse to the law, and when at last justice has settled the claims there is enmity! Hate and evil are in either heart. Spite rules out the Christian graces. There is hardly a community where such a condition does not exist. There may have been recourse to arbitration instead of to the civil courts, but in either case there has been 'suing at the law.' If the party at fault would go to his brother and say: 'You have taken my coat, I acknowledge it to be yours; here is my cloak also; let it be a pledge of peace between us,' how different

I Look Like a Minister's Wife

would be the result! In many cases the original 'coat' would be returned. We do sorely need the giving of the 'cloak,' the meeting more than half way in a dispute, the tangible evidence of that measure of love which 'giveth all things, hopeth all things, endureth all things.'

"How we fall far short of understanding the Master—as if he meant that Mr. By=ends should borrow my overcoat and hasten its already threadbare condition! Mr. By=ends is well=to= do, better able to lend to me than I to him. Because he asks my overcoat, shall I hasten to offer him my other clothing? The question asked so long ago by one who would shirk his duties and have Jehovah's sanction for all the race is a momentous question now: 'Am I my brother's keeper?' Yes, a hundred times over. My brother is what I keep him. I will not keep him a beggar."

CHAPTER XIII

My Neighbors Stop Borrowing

I saw that John was getting the best of the argument; but I liked to prolong it as much as possible, so I said: " But just think of offending these people. They will leave the church perhaps if we are disobliging, or lend their influence against you. Better to keep the peace at all hazards. Mr. By-ends is an officer of the church, you know."

"These people to whom you are loaning your best things do not thank you," John replied. "They esteem you less highly than if you refused. There is no truer aphorism than Shakespeare's own: 'Neither a borrower nor a lender be, for loan oft loses both itself and friend, and borrowing dulls the edge of husbandry.' The borrowing system has ruined many a friendship. It is degrading to both the borrower and lender. Give to the *poor* always, and when by stress of necessity they would cover their alms-needing by the request of a loan, we will lend to them hoping for nothing again, respecting their desire to make returns, of course. 'He that giveth to the poor lendeth to the Lord.' I would

My Neighbors Stop Borrowing

make a parallel passage for that and write, 'He that lendeth to the rich honoreth not the Lord.'"

Just then the door opened and our neighbor, Mrs. Light=of=mind, appeared with her three children. (I shall continue to borrow from Bunyan until I am done with this subject.) She said, "Good morning," and asked if I would "take care of the little ones" while she went to the city. She "would get home before dark if possible," and "would I excuse their appearance?" she had "brought them just as they were without changing their clothes."

I sighed and said, "Certainly," as I had so often done before in the case of many of my neighbors' children. The fact is, I had kept a small orphan asylum on demand and cared for neglected children, feeling in this, as in other matters, that I was "helping John."

John looked at Mrs. Light=of=mind and then at me and then at the three untidy children Then he said: "Mrs. Light=of=mind, will you kindly excuse my wife to-day? She is overworked, I fear. You see she is generous to a fault, and I shall have to persuade her to be content with caring for me and the children."

Again I felt my burdens lightened and a gratifying sense of having a protector between me and imposition. At the same time my long=

My Neighbors Stop Borrowing

schooled but misplaced conception of benevolence was a little shocked. My neighbor went her way and John went his into the study.

Well, I left off loaning except to the poor. It required no small ingenuity sometimes to break myself and my neighbors of the habit. As I intimated, the article returned was at times deficient in quality and so we had been the losers. I was helped a trifle by a hint from an aunt of mine. It is a pity to record so undignified an action on the part of a minister's wife, but it's the truth, and so I tell it.

When Mrs. Ignorance brought back some tea which she had borrowed and I knew it was not the same that we were using, I simply set it up in the cupboard.

The next time Mrs. Ignorance ran in to borrow a little tea for supper I took down her old stock, and in a perfectly innocent way handed it to her, saying: "Certainly; here is the last you brought me; I haven't had occasion to use it." She took it with a slight change of color and did not borrow again.

It was the same with many other things—butter, eggs, flour and sugar. No one could complain if I loaned them their own stock. In some cases I no longer had some "to spare" of a desired article, and in others, as with clothing and household utensils, we were "going to use them

My Neighbors Stop Borrowing

ourselves." It did not take so very long to turn over a new leaf and everybody was the gainer. Nor did I give offense. I had a good-natured, merry sort of manner that smoothed many a rough place.

It is remarkable the amount of borrowing that is done, especially among rural people. They will borrow a thing from a neighbor who lives as far away as the grocery store out of sheer habit. The pity of it is, innocent little children are usually the operators. "Here, Jennie, borrow this," or "Here, Johnnie, borrow that" brings up a child in the way its mother goes. And so we have races of borrowers. I mean generations, not races.

I often told John he had better borrow his sermons from some source and so be on the common plane. But John said that was "meaner than borrowing flour and butter."

As to having so many callers at odd hours from people with no intention but to kill time, John said I must have it understood that "except on three afternoons in the week I was not at home to miscellaneous company." He had a screen with locked door placed around the back entrance, and this gave me my kitchen undisturbed. How much more free I felt, and how much more an independent woman! I regained lost strength and grew young and plump again. I had time

My Neighbors Stop Borrowing

to ride horseback and attend lectures and romp with the children. I wrote an occasional squib for the papers, too, for which I received many a dollar from good-natured editors. In short, I became light-hearted and free. I lost that resemblance to the ordinary minister's wife which had distinguished me the year before.

If this allusion to a very personal experience chances to fall before the notice of a well-meaning, but too much engrossed minister, let him take two looks at his wife the next time they sit down to tea. And if that minister's congregation happens to cast their eyes upon the page before me, let them also take two looks at the minister's wife. All these looks combined may startle the lady, but—results are what we work for.

CHAPTER XIV

Abijah Noseworthy's Wild Oats

During the interval when the church at Sunrise Park had no pastor, individual members kept up the prayer=meeting. Now, a prayer=meeting conducted without a recognized leader, or by a self=appointed leader, is sometimes a thing of distinction. John doubted the wisdom of keeping up such a prayer=meeting, especially when the meeting is held in the church as a public affair. A house=to=house prayer=meeting is different. There is a host, who, with some responsibility is temporary leader, and a meeting of this sort approaches nearer the original type.

At Sunrise Park the weekly prayer=meeting came to be a curious institution. Its tolerated leader was Abijah Noseworthy. He was the law personified. If humanity had justice meted out to it, in his opinion, it would be committed to " endless pangs "—excepting himself, and, when he felt especially magnanimous, a *few* others. He was the "main stand=by" in prayer=meeting. The meeting never "dragged," as the saying is, when he was there.

Abijah Noseworthy's Wild Oats

How well I remember him! Sharp-featured, keen-eyed, a trifle nervous, of firm and emphatic convictions concerning himself, and sometimes concerning others. His eye wandered, or rather dwelt upon every individual before him as if he read them. A happy tone of voice, a trustful, hopeful prayer, was sure to be followed by a testimony from Abijah Noseworthy. And Abijah's testimonies had grown exceedingly personal. When he rose to speak he waved his handkerchief as if it were a signal to warn other barks off the coast. He'd "been there." But he was "safely over." He always pointed to a time in the "far-distant past" with a twirl of his thumb over his right shoulder, when he had been "the chief of sinners."

It was such a long while ago when Abijah Noseworthy was a sinner that one would think the years might have buried it in mercy to his hearers if not to himself. It was in the "far-away past" that Abijah, according to his own testimony, had "sown his wild oats." He had "dipped into the very dregs of sin" to use his own words. I took occasion to inquire into the early history of the man from sheer curiosity, not thinking it possible that such a sinner as he averred himself to have been could have been born and brought up in Sunrise Park. I was assured by more than one veteran as old as

Abijah Noseworthy's Wild Oats

Abijah that he was the son of a deacon, or elder, or some other dignified church official, and that he had been reared in extreme religious severity. He had never been twenty miles from his birthplace, and, to the knowledge of none of his contemporaries, had he ever swerved from the "path of rectitude."

Abijah had never alluded to his "apprenticeship to the devil" as he termed it until he was past sixty. Then, during some revival services when rival testimony was being given of a gruesome type, he suddenly remembered what a sinner he had been.

Whether it was an overwhelming conviction that in some way he had been cheated out of the good times he ought to have had, or that he had been reading the "Power of Religion" and imagined himself to have been in early life a Cardinal Wolsey or a John Wilmot, we never knew. He would rise in prayer-meeting and declare that he had been "worse than anybody present." This was news to his friends, and at first it shocked them. Abijah held up his hands in holy horror of himself. He would put into the densest shade the last speaker who had timidly alluded to his own past sinful career.

" I've been a worse sinner than any of you!" Abijah would exclaim, as if he had suddenly discovered the one thing in which he had ex-

Abijah Noseworthy's Wild Oats

celled. "I've been the blackest of sinners, I say; I was steeped in sin; given over to the adversary; a victim to every sort of wickedness; of every sort, I say."

As time and opportunity continued, Abijah went more into details. He told of how he had been "lost, utterly lost"; and finally of his conversion "in the ball-room." Now, the suggestion of Abijah Noseworthy's ever having indulged in the mazes of the dance, more than once caused a smile to ripple over the faces of the young folks and even the elders exchanged inquiring glances. When he recounted his adventures in a "gambling hell," the plot was of so common and modern a type that distrust was plainly written upon every face.

Suddenly breaking away from the "black past" Abijah would straighten himself and, gazing into the far corner of the sanctuary, exclaim with grave, slow pathos: "But look at me now, my friends! I am a spared monument—a spared monument!"

A curious-looking monument certainly was Abijah Noseworthy. Still he was like a monument, come to think of it, for the history of his sins welded so into his peculiar personal appearance made a lasting memorial of him.

The apparent pride with which he spoke of his sinful career was noticeable. I fancy that if

Abijah Noseworthy's Wild Oats

any one of his hearers had alluded to the man as a victim of early vice, Abijah would scarcely have acquiesced. He was fond of the contrast which he knew by practice so well to make between his imagined "dark past" and his present status. He was "the hardest case" in my opinion that we met with in the new church—so self-complacent; so righteous by comparison; so devoid of charity towards others. But John was hopeful even of him.

By degrees the prayer-meeting took on new shape. John suggested that if any of us had sinned we had better forgive ourselves if we had been forgiven, and not allude to a past which, in the sight of heaven, was as though it had never been. "Shame," he said, "ought to make a man reticent on some points. It is enough that we all have sinned. Keeping ourselves and our neighbors continually in mind of our sins by recounting them is only second to practicing them."

John thought that personal testimony in prayer-meeting has its temptations. He doubted the expediency of frequent allusions to one's personal feelings outside of an occasional reference to the continuance of one's faith. If one feels happy, one's neighbors will notice. Happiness or "low spirits" very much depends upon digestion. One's feelings are no criterion

Abijah Noseworthy's Wild Oats

as to an exemplary life. The fact that a man is peaceful is no proof that he is holy.

If one becomes possessed of a sanctified heart and life the community will recognize the fact as surely as they know that spring has come. It needs no testimony of the lips to convince them. Holiness is luminous of itself; to allude to the possession of it too frequently puts one in a position to be contradicted. It is as if one feared adverse testimony.

To testify as to another's holy life is a different thing. "Let us have more testimony of this sort in prayer=meeting," John would say. "We are all bad enough; none of us is good enough. By their fruits ye shall know them; not by what they say."

The personal pronoun "I" should, for the most part, be relegated to the "closet."

CHAPTER XV
Silas Coombs and Death-bed Scenes

There was another character at Sunrise Park, the exact opposite of Abijah Noseworthy. Silas Coombs was a sunny, hopeful man, of sweet faith and glowing Christianity. He never alluded to his own sins nor to those of anybody else. It is doubtful if he had ever committed any great sins; and it is certain that, in his presence, others forgot their own. To make a man forget his sins is almost equal to making him forsake his sins. By thinking about one's sins overmuch one exaggerates them as he also can his virtues. To turn away from sin is not to have it in mind any more.

In prayer-meeting Silas Coombs was a burning and a shining light. Everybody loved him; the giddy and forward most of all. Did any member discourse upon the sorrows of life and the "purifying influence of grief," Silas Coombs was sure to put a bright side upon it all. "Sometimes I am afraid I am a sinner let alone," he said. "Seems as though I never had any trouble. The sun has been always shining."

Silas Coombs and Death-bed Scenes

And yet we all knew that he had seen many sorrows.

I believe Silas Coombs led more people to the "light" than an ordinary minister, and yet he never preached a sermon. He never prayed in meeting neither, except as he said the Lord's Prayer with the rest. But he must have done a great deal of praying out of meeting, and he prayed with others, too. He would go to the woods nutting, or fishing with the boys. With one boy he would happen to stroll away from the rest, and before the boy knew it he and Silas Coombs would be kneeling on some mossy bank together. It was a surprise to the boy, I am sure, though how far Silas Coombs had contrived the plot nobody knew. It was a picture—the gray-haired man, little and bent of figure, but cheery of face, taking a day's outing with the boys just as if he were a boy himself. Nobody will ever know till the "books are opened" how much that neighborhood owed to Silas Coombs.

He visited the dying with a defined, certain joy in his face that must have daunted Death with its very surety of hope. Often he was sent for, and asked to come, as if his presence were a sort of challenge to the grim messenger. And he always went, hymn-book in hand. No matter whether the person about to pass away were conscious or not, there stood Silas singing

Silas Coombs and Death=bed Scenes

the soul away as if the final issue depended upon his faithfulness.

He seldom asked any questions, but, as he expressed it, " hoped for the best." He was an old=fashioned singer and the words of the ancient tunes were clear.

"On Jordan's stormy banks I stand," floated out at open windows without a quaver. There was assurance in the voice as if " Canaan's fair and happy land " came down to meet " Jordan's stormy banks " on the near side. It came to be a saying: "If Silas Coombs was there the boatman pale waited with his hat off on the farther bank while Silas bore the dying one across and deposited him bodily in 'sweet fields beyond the swelling flood '."

John used to say that when he came to die he wanted Silas Coombs to take him over. "When thou passest through the waters I will be with thee." It is possible for Him to be with thee in the person of Silas Coombs or some other singing saint. Silas will not be on this side to take John over, for he went across himself years ago, too weak to sing—but John sang for him. At the close of the lines " Could we but stand where Moses stood and view the landscape o'er " John stopped, for the look on Silas' calm face assured him that the old man was there in advance of the " flood."

Silas Coombs and Death=bed Scenes

Abijah Noseworthy was also often at the side of the sick and dying, though he was seldom sent for. With his long and disconsolate face he would go gloomily into the sick=room, approach the bedside, sigh, sit down resignedly, and read the account of Dives and Lazarus, dwelling on the torment of Dives with a startling moderation. He always expressed little hope for a happy hereafter, and if he found a dying man hopeful he cautioned him against "feeling too sure," as it was quite "possible for a person to be deceived."

One day Rachel Waterbury came in to ask John to visit the widow Overman's son. He was dying "in great trouble and despair," she said. Abijah Noseworthy had been there and extinguished the last flicker of possibility.

The young man had been something of a prodigal in his late youth, though in his childhood he was gentle and prayerful and full of a child's sweet faith. Away from home "thieves had fallen upon him." He had been wasting in health for a long while and was depressed in mind beyond description. As a culmination of his present troubles Abijah Noseworthy had crossed his path. This "father in Israel" had conscientiously bereft him of what his mother had ardently hoped would be graciously his in a dying hour. John went immediately to see

Silas Coombs and Death=bed Scenes

the young man. The mother met him at the door in an agony of feeling. Her eyes were tearless and so full of unspoken sorrow that John said he could have wept at sight of her. The young man was propped against the pillows, his great sparkling eyes looking out of the window and across the river which meandered softly through the fields.

"I am going," he murmured, "without God and without hope. He says I have sinned away my day of grace. It is written 'My Spirit shall not always strive with man.' It is what I deserve, and yet, and yet——"

What he would have said was hindered by his coughing. "And yet," John said, as if it had been himself that was talking, "Jesus Christ came to give us something better than we deserve. Who says that you have sinned away your day of grace, my brother?"

The young man looked up. "Why, the Bible says it, and that good man says it, and my own heart says it. I feel it. I know it. I cannot even pray; there is no light."

"Has Abijah Noseworthy prayed for you?" asked John.

"No," was the reply, "he said he 'couldn't pray the way I was feeling.' He said there wasn't much doubt I was lost, according to my own testimony. As the tree falls, there it will

Silas Coombs and Death-bed Scenes

lie. He that is unjust let him be unjust still. Mother, go away."

Mrs. Overman was like a being without muscle or power of movement. She stood, straining her eyes at John and clutching at the footboard in the agony of mother-love. "My sister, let us pray," said John. She knelt with him mechanically.

"Our Father," John said, "make thyself known to this thy trustless child. Cast out the demon of doubt and bid him rise even to heaven. Thou art our Father—his Father. Make him assured that when the veil of his flesh is drawn aside he shall see Thee without his flesh; without the sin which has mortified the flesh; without the despair which the very weakness of the flesh has made him heir to. Thou dost love him. Far back in his childhood he was Thy child and of such the Lord himself has said, 'They shall never perish; they are in My hand.' Hold him in Thy hand." And then John read in low, calm tones, that marvelous fifty-third chapter of Isaiah: "Wounded for our transgressions, bruised for our iniquities. All we, like sheep, have gone astray. . . . For the transgression of my people was he stricken. . . . No deceit in his mouth. . . . He shall bear their iniquities. . . . He bore the sin of many."

Silas Coombs and Death=bed Scenes

Then John told the sick man to go to sleep and rest a while and he would come again in the morning.

John was so cheerful through and through that he infected this young man, naturally. Those who are already sick are so susceptible to infection. They take everything that is offered them from sheer inability to reject it. It was not long before doubt and despair were bounding away in the distance like wolves pursued.

"How can anyone help having faith in Jesus," John said, "when Jesus, by the very gift of himself, proved his faith in man? Christ did not doubt that the world would be saved. How then can that world doubt the power of Christ to save?" "And what is faith to a human heart if it cannot itself make faith for another? I will have faith for you," John said. "You are in pain. You have been so long in pain that you have forgotten what it is to be well. You can think of nothing but that pain and its counterpart, the evil which was in you for so long. You are weary alike of the sin and the pain. You are sorry for the sin; it makes the pain sharper. But see, Jesus Christ came into the world to save sinners. Let Him bear away your sin in His own way; in His own way He will also bear away the pain. Trust

Silas Coombs and Death-bed Scenes

Him, and when the pain and the sin are both gone you will clasp hands with Jesus and go singing of faith forever."

And so John held the light while Frank Overman went over the river. Just before he stepped down the gentle slope he turned to his mother and said: "It's all right," and John echoed, "It's all right."

JOHN HELD THE LIGHT WHILE FRANK OVERMAN WENT OVER THE RIVER.

CHAPTER XVI

The Church has a Revival

As to "death-bed repentances" John says a man ought to be ashamed who doubts. That someone repents on his supposed death-bed, recovers, and repents that he did repent, is no reason for anyone to conclude that the repentance was not genuine. Such an excuse is brought up again and again by men who are too narrow to admit of widening. Had the repentant passed on into the certainty of sight he would have been remorseful that his repentance was so tardy. Instead of passing on into perfect sight he tarried in the same condition that had blinded him in the past. It is the vision of to-day that moves most of us to repent to-day. "Lord remember me," cried the thief in the extremity of despair. And the answer came swiftly, outrunning the despair, "To-day thou shalt be with Me in Paradise." To-morrow the pain and weakness and revolt of the flesh might postpone faith. Another day, when there is no to-morrow for the flesh, faith will be born never to die.

As to "dying in one's sins" John says we have no right to pass judgment in a single case.

The Church has a Revival

Someone has said that dying is like climbing to a mountain top. Almost out of breath in the ascent, quite out of breath at the summit, the traveler falls on his face deaf to our cries, dumb as to the expression of his own thoughts. We, waiting in the valley below, conclude that the ascent has wrought no change because, forsooth, we did not note it. We would fain climb, too, but we cannot now. We shall have our turn by and by and alone.

Waiting, below the mountain, we have no right to say of the receding soul, "He sees nothing; he feels nothing," simply that his sight and speech are sealed to us. What he sees beyond the crest, what he hears from the other side, we may not know; it is his secret. John says "a second is time enough to ravish the sight when the film of the flesh is falling like scales from eyes that have never seen." He would never preach any soul into despair because men could see only despair. His comrades and the church folk had known the thief all his life. They "knew he had never repented." They were away about their own affairs when he died. They did not hear the little word that passed between him and heaven on the mountain crest. And they would no doubt disbelieve the record when they saw it. "Haven't we known that man?" they would say. "As the tree falls, there will it lie." "My

The Church has a Revival

Spirit shall not always strive with man." "That thief has sinned out his day of grace. He always ridiculed us when we wanted to talk with him about his soul."

We forget that "the secret of the Lord is with men," dying men, perhaps. We would deny others the "secret" because we ourselves have not participated. The "bread and water of life" may be rejected for very lack of hunger until the last moment. We deny that they may be partaken of, because perchance they are not taken from our hand. "Stolen water is sweet and bread eaten in secret is pleasant." The water of life, stolen, snatched from receding opportunity; the bread of life eaten in the narrow passage betwixt two worlds may be very "pleasant," and that late communion seal the covenant.

Not that John recommended death=bed repentance to anyone who had time for other. He would only make the church more charitable, less certain of despair for those who die and leave no sign. "There shall no sign be given unto them" in some cases. There is a sort of religious conceit in the way some sober people cant their heads and look hopeless, and say of someone, "I have talked with him a great many times and I never got any satisfaction. Let it be a warning to others." Usually such men are arbitrary. They mete out justice to their little

The Church has a Revival

children with a swing of the switch, their wives are continually reminded "that they are to be subject to their own husbands," and in church affairs they meet backsliders with threats. Being full of conceit themselves, and arbitrary, they imagine the Heavenly Father to be like them.

The first winter we were at Sunrise Park the church people proposed a revival. Revivals were in the air. There was one in almost every church and it seemed natural that we should have one, too. John acquiesced, but not cordially. He is conservative on the revival question. He says it is "the Lord's work whenever a soul seeks the light," but the credit is given to Brothers So= and=So who have a great reputation as revivalists.

Well, we had the revival. The "Evangelist" in charge was a youngish man of some ability and undoubted Christian experience. But he labored under mistakes. John is looking over my shoulder and says kindly that I "ought to be very careful in speaking of this young man, for some of his descendants may be living and they would take it to heart if I criticised too sharply. Besides, it is like putting one's hand to 'steady the ark' when one attempts to speak of revivals. One is apt to go too far and say what had better not be said."

IT WAS AS IF HE WAS "TAKING STOCK."

The Church has a Revival

Now, with all due respect for John, and the hope that I shall not offend one of the "descendants" referred to, I am going to tell all about that revival. I believe in revivals but not in some ways of conducting them. I do not mean to be sweeping, however.

The day and hour came. The "Evangelist" took his seat and let his eye dwell upon the faces before him. It was as if he were "taking stock," so to speak. He seemed to be calculating how many "assistants" he might expect from the somewhat varied sea of faces, expectant, incredulous, sombre, resigned, and repellent. After due preliminaries he proceeded to inform his hearers that at the last place where he "labored" he had been the means of saving forty-two souls. "The humble means," he added in parentheses. He then appealed to "the saved" to come boldly out and "help" him. "As many as were willing to do so would please stand on their feet."

Now, this "Evangelist" was a stranger in the place. How could he know that two-thirds of "the saved" who pledged themselves to "help" him that day were men and women of little reputation? But so it was. To be sure there were no very "black sheep" among them; that is, they were not criminals in the common sense; and they were church members. Yet they were

The Church has a Revival

defective in reputation. Some of them were, or had been recently, "a little off," as the saying is, on "side issues." They had dipped into "Christian Science," tried "Spiritualism," been disciples of the last "Faith Cure," or turned prophets as to coming "religious wars" and the speedy "end of the world." A few had permitted the temptations of business life to sear their consciences by way of small gains that had better not have been. Other few were "kicking against the pricks" by way of avoiding small debts and minor obligations—trifles to be sure, but sufficient to soil "the white robe of a child of Jesus."

Like such people in many another community these were first to pledge themselves to "help" the Evangelist. Had he been the teacher of *any* "new doctrine" it would have been the same. There are eager souls who are ready to be "filled with new wine" of whatsoever sort. Patched up for the occasion these "old bottles" are not recognized by the Evangelist and so "the wine of the kingdom" is "spilled." Of course, the more dignified, substantial, always-the-same church members knew at a glance that they "couldn't work with that crowd," and so they kept their seats. If that Evangelist had known as much of human nature as he ought to have known he would have asked the first

The Church has a Revival

volunteers to fall back and bear the cross in the rear. The very persons who kept their seats and hence were the subjects of severe censure as being "cold," "lukewarm," "doubting Thomases," etc., were really the "backbone" of that church. They knew very well that the Evangelist had made his first mistake, but to rectify it was impossible.

However, there were "conversions" and "higher experiences." No one but the Evangelist knew exactly how many; he kept a strict account. He thought he was counting right, but how could he know that nearly all of those "higher experiences" claimed under his persuasive reign had been in the possession of the same claimants off and on for years? They kept them, like their best clothes, to bring out and dust up and wear every time a revival came their way. Yes, indeed! There were people in our church who always had "higher experiences."

The Evangelist every now and then alluded to the "stars" he wanted for his "crown." And he already had a good many. He was like the quack doctors who cure cases given up by "the best physicians." Very bad people had accidentally come under his influence and were converted; people who had resisted "every other evangelist and preacher." He told wonderful

The Church has a Revival

stories of these conversions. They were as thrilling as the stories of adventure paid for by the line in the newspapers. Always the Evangelist himself figured largely in the foreground. He insisted on everybody being converted in a certain way. Unless a sinner consented to be saved by certain methods quite to the revivalist's satisfaction there was a "lost soul" in the case. And they must "confess" in just his way, also, or they were not right. Sometimes he would get all the converts kneeling around, and the good people praying for them, all believing the Evangelist was praying, too. I saw him take a notebook from his pocket and looking about upon the prostrate forms before him, count them, as a herdsman counts his herd, and jot the number down. At the close of the revival he had quite a "showing" in round numbers which he read aloud as the result of two weeks' labors, adding at last it was "all through Grace." At the same time he stroked his beard in a self-complacent manner which gave one the impression that he had been at least the "right-hand man of Grace." Then he plead for "a few more," "just a few more souls" to swell the number to a certain figure, very much as an auctioneer proclaims the bid which he expects.

"Oh, the egotism of it all! the farce upon the

The Church has a Revival

work of the Spirit which is like leaven hid in the meal, or the grain of mustard seed springing to a new life under the surface and rising toward heaven silently!" That is what John said one day.

"But John," I answered, "think of all the good that has been done at revival meetings. And look at the revivalists themselves. Many of them have been taken out of the mire and the clay. And a man has a right to count his gain, be it gold or land or immortal souls, hasn't he? You wouldn't do away with revivals would you?"

"No, indeed," John answered, "but I would not have evangelists count their converts as if they had a copyright on souls, or as if they drew a certain commission on "new hearts." The disciples started out on that line, but the Lord reproved them by telling them to rejoice rather that their own names were written in heaven. The Master knew how great would be the temptation to tell in Samaria what they had done in Galilee. He knew there would be a disposition to count the possible stars in advance of the crown."

Our revivalist donned the guise of Abijah Noseworthy, and in his seeming solicitude for others deemed it his duty to describe the exact compound of the mire and the clay out of which

The Church has a Revival

he had been drawn. At the close of one such discourse, when the confession of the Evangelist somewhat resembled bravado, I overheard a young man say to another as they walked arm-in-arm from the church door: "My stars, Sam, I never sunk so deep in sin as that; guess I'll wait a while till I'm more like the preacher. Make a greater contrast, you see, and then I can tell as big a yarn as he can." And the two walked away laughing at what they thought a good joke.

After the meetings closed the church settled down on very much its old footing. The members who had professed the "higher experience" folded it away to be fresh and new when the next revival should warm them up. As to the new converts, I admit there were one or two, but by far the greater number went the old way. It was good to have two or three, but how much greater results would have been obtained by different methods!

John sighed when it was all over. There was a reaction in the church. If evangelists could be settled for life in one place, and themselves work out the problems which they suggest, it might be better. Our revivalist went his way somewhat richer than he came. Just before the close, when the excitement was at the highest pitch, some brother, after a whispered

The Church has a Revival

interview with the leader, proposed that there be a subscription taken up for the good man. "The workman is worthy of his meat." Gold rattled and silver clinked and pennies jingled. There was a goodly sum of money raised "to defray expenses." "Defraying expenses" is a perennial excuse for asking alms for the revivalist. "Without money and without price" is Salvation to be had. And yet—I was going to say something about a pretty good price, but I desist. I will say, however, that it will be a "golden era" when not a copper is asked for during a revival meeting. Let the church see to it that new converts are not asked to give "according to the blessing they have received."

CHAPTER XVII
Church Gossip

In the matter of church gossip John was very conservative. He was averse to family gossip, neighborhood gossip, and all kinds of idle talk, chitter-chatter, "profane and vain babbling" as the Scripture terms it. "Worst of all," he said, "is church gossip; pulpit babbling."

And yet, here I am writing a whole book of gossip—and church gossip, at that. I am inconsistent. The very thing I deplore I am doing. But I have an object. To gossip with an object, and that a worthy one, is to rob gossip of its hatefulness—and yet I feel guilty all the time I am doing it.

"How dreadful it is," John used to say, "to hear a minister descant upon the erroneous creeds or practices of sister churches, making these the subject of an occasional discourse; or to enliven his sermons with stray bits of fault-finding, sufficient to arouse just a little animosity in his hearers. For my part," he said, "I expect to meet a long line of bishops and priests, both Christian and heathen, in the New Jerusalem, and throw my arms around their

Church Gossip

necks, forgetting everything but the fact that each and all are forgiven their sins. We pine for heaven's freedom, but the chains of our distinctive doctrines prevent our seeing the Angel that is waiting to unloose our fetters. Love is the Angel."

John made friends with all the ministers of whatever creed—so they loved the Lord Jesus. He said there was "help and farther sight and uplifting of spirit in such association." Once I opened the study door, thinking John had gone down town, and there were John and a Catholic priest kneeling side by side. Not that John "leaned toward the Catholics" as the saying is, but he had love in his heart. Love is attractive, not repellent, and it attracts its own kind. John says "no man can preach Jesus and be altogether wrong."

"Why, John," I would answer, "doesn't the Bible read that many shall say at the last day, 'Have we not prophesied in Thy name and done many wonderful things?' And the Lord will answer, 'I never knew you.'"

John replies, "I said no man can preach Jesus and be altogether wrong. I made no reference to prophecies, nor to casting out devils, nor to doing wonderful things. There are many who do these things, but who do not preach Jesus. Prophets are almost as thick as

Church Gossip

stars. They make doleful predictions as to the 'end of the world,' approaching 'tribulation,' and 'clashing of arms.' They read Daniel and the Revelations in a sombre tone, as if their mission were to make people nervous and expectant of ill, and full of dread. The doctrine of Jesus is the doctrine of peace and forgiveness and everlasting safety. Having Jesus we do not shudder at prophecy. There are other impostors who work upon the fancy of their victims. For a show of good, and to gain confidence, they feign calling upon the Name of the Lord. They cast out devils, or say they do, and work miracles, and heal diseases, and do wonders. But the Lord takes no notice, unless to be sorry. 'I never knew you' will be his reception of their protestations. To preach Jesus, to point men to Him, to teach the world that there is a fair prospect of its meeting Him face to face one day—all this is different."

I came to think with John in regard to the love there ought to be between churches and believers. I suppose we can no more help differences than we can change our individual features, and yet we could be more alike in love.

It is said that modern surgery restores lost family likeness by interference. Here a tiny slit, and there a stretch, and on this side the di-

Church Gossip

viding of a muscle, and the lineaments are changed. They are induced to approach some ancestral model. Make the application fit the churches and church members.

John used to say there is "a distinction between sin and the sinner. It was the sin that was borne away into the wilderness; the sinner was left in the camp. We close the Old Testament and carry out the sinners to be stacked heaven high or publicly whipped. We rub our holy hands and give thanks that the days of church riots are over. Would that we had buried the spirit of strife so that it, with the body of dissension, might have seen corruption! Instead of fagots we use religious newspapers; and in place of pitch, church ostracism, which is equally adhesive. And we use all sorts of strictures, like fetters. We have so swaddled the church that it has no room to grow, and it never is any bigger unless it bursts its bands in places; then it grows irregularly, and so much by piecemeal that the body is full of humps and contortions and disproportionate members. We are too impatient of one another. Let Judas alone and he will go and hang himself. There is no need of haste on our part in building his gallows."

The Lord himself set an example of patience and tolerant communion. They say it is

Church Gossip

worry that makes one grow old and wrinkled. Worry is what makes the church wrinkled. Abijah Noseworthy used to worry a good deal. He worried lest the young folks go too fast, and the old folks too slow. He was never tired of lamenting that the "ancient days were better than these," and if he saw anybody hopeful in regard to the progress of the church, he was sure to throw cold water.

I forgot to mention Abijah's wife when I was speaking of him. She was her husband's other self. She had been an invalid for years, but there was none of the cheer and sweetness in her presence one often meets in the sick-room. Everybody went to see her out of curiosity, or from duty, or in sweet charity. Somehow Mistress Noseworthy picked up all the church gossip that was floating in the air and communicated it from church to church. She was not malicious—far from it. She simply dwelt on trouble of any sort, and being of a religious turn of mind it was naturally religious trouble that she dwelt upon. She knew exactly what minister was not "just in accord" with his congregation, and what proportion were in favor of him. She had an innocent way of getting at church secrets when no one suspected her intentions, and she certainly found out some things by sheer intuition. What she knew she

Church Gossip

did not tell as so much slander or gossip, but with deep sighs and, I must believe, real sorrow, she mentioned the "deplorable matter."

Each church in town knew the standing of every other church, and the most pitiable part of it was that trouble of any sort, actual or prophesied, was sure to be exaggerated.

What a life the two must have led!—Abijah Noseworthy and his wife. Nobody ever heard them laugh, nor yet were they seen to cry. Laughter and tears are too near of kin for them ever to have indulged in either. The unmistakable fact that death was "on their track" made them miserable, if they ceased to think of others long enough to consider their personal situation. The fear that "dying grace" would not be granted them tortured the two beyond description.

When his wife actually came "to the brink," Abijah Noseworthy stood by her, the perspiration like great beads rolling down his face, and almost screamed in his distress. "Hold on, Abigail, hold on!" "Wrestle, Abigail, wrestle till the break of day!" And Abigail "wrestled" till at last her features sank into the peace which they had never known in life.

CHAPTER XVIII
At the Women's Meeting

They were a band of loving, earnest, helpful women. They were full of faith in humble enterprises which could lift human kind. They were a part of the wall, so to speak, of the church proper. They bore their share of the burdens which leaned heavily, roof-like, upon the main structure. They were not preachers nor deaconesses nor nuns. They were simply women; some rich, some poor, some with neither poverty nor riches to move them nor to hinder them. Mostly they were housekeepers, snatching these few hours from other cares that they might help in the saving of the world.

On the afternoon I am reporting they had met to cut and sew and make garments for the poorest in the church, or the needy outside of the church. We had been sociably discussing many topics, as women will, while our fingers flew. We had considered individual cups for the Communion service, and actually planned a way to purchase them, provided we could gain the consent of the officials to substitute them

At the Women's Meeting

for the two or three silver goblets then in use. We had sighed that our children, who "loved the Lord Jesus in sincerity," must of necessity be left at home or sit regretfully by our side, while we, who loved the Lord no more than they, had part at his table. Then we discussed the Sunday newspaper, and the selling of cigarettes to minors, and the feeding and clothing of our children, and many other things of mutual interest. There was the decorating of the church. We discussed the question of using tissue paper roses when the summer flowers were gone. On this we all agreed that it is vulgar taste and we voted out the very suggestion. All but Mrs. McEllen had spoken; she was silent. "What is your opinion?" asked Miss Waterbury.

"Oh," replied the lady addressed, with a deep sigh, "I was not thinking of the question before the house, as they say in Congress, but of the pressing needs of our foreign missions."

Every other woman looked up from her work with a smile and a glance around the circle. Mrs. McEllen was "labeled," so to speak, "Foreign Missions." She bore the mark as officers wear their uniforms. It was she who underscored the word "foreign" in the church notices, so that the minister would give the proper

At the Women's Meeting

inflection when he announced a meeting of "the board."

The subject was a sad burden upon her shoulders. I say "sad burden," for she always sighed heavily when she mentioned the matter. She was ever begging for foreign missions, always nudging her neighbors concerning them, and foreign missions were served regularly at her table without so much as variety in the sauce which flavored them. Her Sabbath=school class devoted itself to foreign missions before the little things had learned the beatitudes, or what became of the children who "mocked" an old white head.

Mrs. McEllen button=holed her gentlemen friends for funds to send to India and Japan. She got the funds, too, for the subscription paper in her hand reflected the resolution in her face. She could move an audience to tears by her appeals in behalf of China's womenfolk meandering painfully about on dolls' feet, or Mohammedan girls suffering for fresh air behind closely drawn veils.

Mrs. McEllen, pouring over the last Missionary Journal, was quite unconscious of the fact that her daughter Arabella, was upstairs in tears over the pain in her sensible broad foot as she pushed it into its new number two shoe. She did not suspect that the vision of her other

At the Women's Meeting

daughter, Isabella, was growing defective in consequence of peering between and through the irregular dots in her fashionable veil, nor that she was at that very moment adjusting her new corsets with the lacing thrown around the handle of the door to insure a snug fit.

Isabella was growing pale and her mother noted it with solicitation. Again and again the girl had assured her friends that she did not lace, at the same time drawing in her breath and compressing the pit of her stomach to show that she could indeed "shove her hand up under her corset." Isabella had been designed from her birth for a foreign missionary, and her mother sighed when she looked at her slim figure and sunken eyes.

Mrs. McEllen was "whole-souled," that is, her whole soul was absorbed in this one question, and I am not disparaging the question. It was all right for her to be interested in foreign missions. But for the fact that she overlooked home missions so entirely, I should have nothing to say about her. Indeed, I have nothing to say *against* her as it is. I would simply give what I can remember of the conversation of a small circle of loving, faithful women who met in the church parlors.

As I said, the other ladies exchanged glances when Mrs. McEllen mentioned foreign missions.

At the Women's Meeting

Good-natured glances, of course, for these women had no unkind thought for anyone on that particular day.

"Don't you think," asked Miss Waterbury, "that we have home missions of interest?"

Mrs. McEllen bit off her thread, wet her thimble finger, pinned her work to her knee and sighed. Then she said: "My calling is for foreign missions. I should have been a foreign missionary myself but for the accident of meeting Mr. McEllen. I promised to wed him before I thought to ask his opinion of my cherished mission. Then of course it was too late; but I have laid one daughter at least upon the altar. As to home missions, what is there in the humdrum, tame scenes about us to suggest any kind of mission? Sabbath-school is all right; mothers' meetings, prayer circles, church services of all sorts—they are but fuel for the altar of foreign missions. Aside from these, what is there to absorb you or me? I ask you ladies in the name of heathen lands, and their absolute claim upon us, what is there in Sunrise Park worthy of the name of home missions?"

Mrs. McEllen grew almost eloquent in her appeal, and she threw her scissors down on the table with a sharp click by way of extra emphasis.

Miss Waterbury arose and drank some water.

At the Women's Meeting

The ladies had nodded to her by way of request that she speak.

"I did not drink," she said, "preparatory to a speech. I was thirsty. But I will say that I do see much and many things about us worthy of the name of mission. For instance, there is the Children's Home. How many of us have contributed either money or labor to that? You ought to go there and see those babies, orphans but for Mr. and Mrs. Goodspeed, who adopted them. Do you think it takes no money or care to house them and clothe them, and feed them five or six times a day? No pains to keep them clean and wholesome and well? Where does the money come from for their support? Faith laid the foundation in the hearts of Mr. and Mrs. Goodspeed and love for babies of the race for whom Christ died chinks the crevices as they go along. There is no gold behind the love which prompts this benevolence—only the gold that is in my pocket and yours to be drawn upon as we are prompted by love. The Home began, and grows, feebly. Every dollar received by the managers and the proceeds of their labor go to those babies. They are not *their* babies more than yours or mine; they are God's babies. The whole burden falls upon those two. It makes me blush for us, church women that we

At the Women's Meeting

are. We drop our tears over the hard times of heathen women, who, perchance, carry a few sticks on their backs or are denied the promiscuous companionship of the other sex, of necessity flirting with their own husbands and brothers because denied the luxury of new acquaintances."

Mrs. More spoke next. She said: "I have been thinking of the Rescue Home for Fallen Women. It is not the first one of its kind, you know. Jesus of Nazareth was the first rescue home for the Magdalene. We forget the reformed girl in our zeal for the reformed young man. *He* is in everybody's heart. No need of a rescue home for him. There is hardly a woman of us who would not welcome to her pew on Sunday morning the young man in broadcloth who last year ruined our neighbor's daughter. We may not have been acquainted with that neighbor nor even have seen her daughter; but they are both our neighbors, nevertheless. I say we would welcome the young man to our pew provided he is reformed. We would point him out as a spared monument of grace. Matrons would be overcordial in his reception at the church social, and we would look sweet and affable while he escorted our daughter to supper at a cosy *tete-a-tete* table. They 'would have a good influence over him,' you know. Oh, yes, the

At the Women's Meeting

reformed young man is a lion; there is a career before him and his class. But where is our neighbor's daughter, the victim of the young man's delay in reformation? No son of ours conducts her to a church supper because *she* is reformed. No family pew invites *her* to its conspicuous protection. We pity the women of the foreign harem because perchance the harem is far away. What shall we do for the women of the harems at our door? Can we wash our hands in innocency while we do not rescue the perishing who are crouching at our doors, or who leer at us scarlet-clothed from behind half-drawn blinds?"

This speech and appeal was the cause of quite a flutter among the pocket-handkerchiefs and called to mind a number of instances during the year when a little timely help might have reformed some young woman in our very town.

Mrs. Home was then asked to speak as to minor services of missions. Mrs. Home was the lady who had protested against the supplying of missionary boxes with worn-out clothing, and had besought the generously inclined to "not cut the buttons from garments donated to the destitute."

"Well," she said, "if you wish me to mention some simple way by which to do mission work, I will mention the church supper. Why not

At the Women's Meeting

give what is left to the poor? I don't mean the crumbs and crusts and 'chicken feed' generally, but good, whole cakes and loaves and salads. Ever so many people around us never see a frosted loaf the whole year through save as they peep in, with eyes that water, at the bakery window. Suppose we should make such our guests for once, even if we do not sell twenty-five-cent tickets toward church repairs. There are other church repairs than such as pertain to carpets and pews and curtains and furnaces. Did you notice that poor, oddly dressed old lady some-one brought to our last church supper? I pitied the woman so! and I thought how we stared at her —as if she were out of place. Oh, I do think we ought each to bring some such sister and make her know that we do not see her shawl, nor dress, we are so glad to see her very self. What was it the Master said about the matter —'When thou makest a feast call not thy rich neighbors nor thy kinfolk nor thy friends, but call the poor, the maimed, the halt and the blind?'"

"I, too, have thought of the same thing," remarked another lady. "I am going to do a little gossiping. Don't look startled. The other day I saw a tired, poor old woman on the street with a bundle of clothes in her arms to be washed for somebody. Miss Waterbury drove

At the Women's Meeting

along in her new top buggy and took the old woman to her home, soiled clothes and all. Oh, there might be more 'Sweet Chariots' swinging low for the poor. They greet us at every turn; not the very destitute who are starving, but the common poor who never have a ride in a nice carriage, nor a pudding with plums in it. I saw that same lady (and she needn't blush) wash the dirty face of a child one day, and he was not a relation of hers, neither. He came around with a few miserable peaches and apples to sell. Miss Waterbury told him to wait a minute and she would make him so trim people would *have* to buy his fruit. Then she washed his face and brushed his hair and made a gay butterfly under his chin as if she had done nothing but arrange little boys' neckties all her life. And if you'll believe it she actually wiped that child's feet after he had washed them at the pump. She acted as if she really loved him. I tell you it's these things that tell when we talk of the lack of opportunity in home missions."

Then Mrs. Mayberry said that, as we were gossiping, she might as well tell her story: "I was visiting a lady the other day who was moaning because she had never been able to bring a single soul to Christ, she had 'so much to do at home.' And yet that very night and every night her

At the Women's Meeting

four little ones devoutly kneel by their bedside and pray to 'Our Father who art in heaven,' of whom they would have never known but for that same mother who declares sadly that she has 'never been able to save any souls.' I know of a good many mothers who sigh for a turn at reaping in the fields that are white unto the harvest. They have read the twenty-fifth chapter of Matthew, with streaming eyes that they have so few opportunities of ministering to the Lord. Little ones pull at their skirts and tease for supper, or they awaken in the night with their importunate cries for 'Water, mamma, water.' If these mothers would listen to Him who said 'Whosoever shall give to drink unto one of these little ones a cup of cold water only, he shall in no wise lose his reward,' what a recognition of home missions there would be! John Chinaman, bringing the basket of clean clothes to our kitchen door, is neglected, tolerated perhaps, for the money and hard work he saves us by his washing. We will send the Bible to his wife and children in heathen lands, and when he goes home he will hear them read it, wondering why we never told him anything about it. And yet it is far easier to reach a Chinaman in America or England than to reach him at home."

It was dark; the ladies folded away their work

At the Women's Meeting

and disbanded. On the veranda I heard Mrs. McEllen say to Miss Waterbury: "I wish you would come and see me often. You have done me so much good." And I smiled while I thought of the pressing needs of home missions.

CHAPTER XIX

Was it a Foundling?

There is a mystery about women which I cannot understand. We are one thing at one time and so different at another time. Now, at that meeting which I recorded in the last chapter we were good and true, if not harmonious. How one week changed us! All there is of the resentful, and uncharitable, and unwomanly was rife in the next meeting. It seems that sometimes the spirit of hate for her own sex takes possession of a woman, and she is temporarily deranged. Even good women forget themselves and join in the mad chorus against a little sister, until we may well be convinced that only heaven pities and forgives. At the meeting to which I now refer there was a more general attendance of the ladies, and as I said they were "out of harmony" for no particular reason but—that women will be so.

"It's a terrible thing for her father," said Mrs. A., changing her chair to the west window. "He ought to have put her out to work."

"They say she cries all the time," quoth Mrs.

Was it a Foundling?

B., "and I should think she would cry, the shameless creature."

"She's young to have gone to the bad," chimed in Mrs. C., "and to think of her bringing up the younger children! The whole family is disgraced. I've told my Jennie to have nothing to do with her ever since her mother died. I've felt it in my bones that she was no better than she ought to be."

"They do say she is real modest," said Mrs. D., "and as for work, she's always up before daylight and the house is as neat as a pin. I suppose she is like the 'whited sepulchre' the Bible tells about—fair outside but inside full of corruption. It's a wonder she hasn't contaminated all our children."

The last speaker was a young woman who had become a mother all too soon after a hasty marriage ceremony. Her child was considered respectable, and Mrs. D. herself was a pillar in the Missionary Society. What she said influenced the circle a good deal, I could see. They had all expressed their minds except Rachel Waterbury. She hadn't said a word, nor had I. I was too shocked to say anything. Not shocked at what was being said, but at the danger our Susie had been in, for she had been a schoolmate of Minnie Brown and thought a great deal of her.

Minnie Brown, the subject of all these hard

Was it a Foundling?

things which had been said, was scarcely sixteen. Her mother had died two years before, leaving the young girl to assume her place. Minnie was sweet and winsome, neither bold nor bad, and she made a great many friends. The praise of her was in everybody's mouth until this dreadful mishap, and now the blame of her was on everybody's lips.

The boy lover, not more than eighteen or twenty, had been sent away somewhere, nobody knew where—to college some said, or to Germany. His family were wealthy, though it was said the young man loved Minnie and would have wedded her gladly had he not been prevented by his friends. His father offered Seth Brown five hundred dollars to help him "tide over the misfortune," he said. But Brown refused it.

"He'll need it fast enough with such a girl on his hands," said the lover's father; "what an awful thing it must be to have such a daughter! Couldn't have been brought up right. If he won't take the five hundred dollars, I wash my hands of the whole affair. As for having my son pestered either by the girl or by the neighborhood, that's out of the question. Thank fortune I've money enough to keep him in good society. He need never be seen here again."

When I got home from meeting that day I

Was it a Foundling?

told John the whole story, and when I was done he actually wiped the tears from his eyes. He kissed Susie, who happened to be in the hallway, and started straight for Seth Brown's.

John was an own brother to every man, woman and child in any sort of trouble, but I told him he ought to draw the line between trouble and shame. It doesn't hurt a man to sympathize with trouble, but shame is like pitch; it sticks to anything it touches. "There's danger, John, there's danger," I said to him many times; but he made answer, "I can see no difference between trouble and shame. The Lord bore our shame till the world spat in His face. If they had but turned their backs on Him, as they might on me; but they couldn't turn their backs on Him. And the Lord hath laid on himself the iniquity of us all. He was put to open shame, despising the shame."

It was of no use to argue with John—as well think of arguing with the sun when it shines or with the wind when it blows.

Time passed and the days were dark at Seth Brown's. When the baby came, some of the ladies of the Missionary circle went to the house "to set things straight," they said.

Minnie was too distressed to object to anything, though they did all their talking right before her, and she told Rachel Waterbury

Was it a Foundling?

afterwards that she "remembered every word they said, and would through all eternity."

"It's a pity the little thing cannot die," said one. "Is she well, nurse?"

"Is it deformed at all?" asked another. "It's a wonder it isn't, as a just judgment."

"Don't let her have it for a minute," said a third. "She might love it, and then we couldn't do anything with her, you know."

"The best thing to do with it is to give it away as soon as possible," said another lady. "I don't suppose any of the families around here would run such a risk as to take an unfortunate infant like this."

"Nobody would take it who knew the circumstances," said another; "the only thing left for us to do, as a body of respectable women acting in the place of the girl's dead mother, is to take it to the Foundlings' Home. I'm willing to take it there myself though I don't see how I can spare the time. But I feel willing to rid the neighborhood of such a calamity."

I was younger then than I am now, but that is hardly an excuse for my silence on that occasion. I was there and heard it all. My cheeks burn with shame whenever I think of it. I, the minister's wife, who ought to have taken that poor motherless girl and her innocent baby to

Was it a Foundling?

my breast—I, to sit by and hear all that! I was weak; worse than weak, I was wicked; and I shall never forgive myself, not even when I meet Minnie face to face in heaven, if I get there after what I know of myself.

And so it was agreed to send the sweet, pink baby to the Foundlings' Home. Yes, it was sweet. It looked just as if the angels might have kissed it, in spite of its fate. Ah, its fate! If I only knew its fate! If I could only find that baby, and love it, and keep it safe for Minnie, the broken-hearted mother! But I shall never see that baby until I meet it at the last judgment. And then, how can I look into its eyes?

When they carried the baby out, Minnie, the little mother, stretched out her hands and tried to say something; but she was "out of her head," the nurse said, and nobody paid any attention to her. I did suggest that we wait until she got well and could help us to decide; but the rest all declared that Minnie had "no right to say anything;" that she was "only a girl" and not a "married woman;" that "in the end she would come to see it was not best to burden herself and the family with an illegitimate child."

The father of Minnie's lover kindly sent his closed carriage around to the house to convey one of the ladies and the child to the Found-

Was it a Foundling?

lings' Home. He said we were doing "just right." That it "would blast Minnie's prospects, and leave an everlasting stigma on her name to have the child around."

The women all agreed to give the wayward girl a chance to reform, "now that this stumbling-block of a child was out of the way."

When I got home I found Rachel Waterbury talking with John. She and John had grown to be great friends. They were always planning how to help the poor and shiftless and sorrowful. I didn't think they quite knew what they were doing; at least I told them they did not stop to consider the impression they were making on respectable society. Miss Waterbury carried peace and rest to all the crowd of unfortunates, as surely as some people carry bread and chicken to the poor. The bread and chicken are usually in a basket, while the peace and rest I mentioned were in Miss Waterbury's loving personal presence. When I came in she was saying to John: "The family are in comfortable circumstances, and I think it would be better for the girl to keep the baby. It is hers. Hadn't you better see Minnie's father and persuade him to refuse to let it be taken away?"

"It's too late," I ventured to say, "it's gone to the Foundling Asylum."

Was it a Foundling?

"It's no foundling," answered John, with more spirit than usual. "Webster defines a foundling to be 'A deserted or exposed infant. A child found without a parent or owner.' They have no more right to call that child a foundling, and to take it away without its mother's consent than if the baby belonged to us. Talk about the girl's shame! Shame on the Missionary Committee!"

I was speechless. I had never seen John like this before.

Miss Waterbury rose to go. "I had no idea," she said, "that they would hurry the matter so. I would have taken the baby home myself till the poor child-mother was responsible. But as you say, it's too late. I am going to see Minnie; she shall never want a friend."

And Miss Waterbury stayed with Minnie as long as she lived. She fell into quick consumption and died in two months.

The other ladies called occasionally to read and pray with her and to "help her reform," as they said. But they had "other charitable cases and could not stay long at a time—besides, women with families of their own should not go too often to such a place. It is all right to help fallen girls, but one must be careful."

Minnie never ceased to cry for her baby, and

Was it a Foundling?

once Rachel and I went to the Foundlings' Home to find it, but it could never be identified—a precaution of the Missionary Committee, I suppose.

"Miss Waterbury," Minnie would say, "God gave me my baby. It was my baby. Why did they take it away? I want my baby. Those ladies come here and pray God to forgive my sin. He forgave my sin long before the baby came."

After a while she died. When we came to the grave we found that someone had set up at the head a white cross of lilies and roses. Attached to the right arm of the cross was a card with the inscription, "Neither do I condemn thee," signed, "Jesus." I believe John or Miss Waterbury placed it there, but nobody ever knew. Just as the casket was lowered into the grave Miss Waterbury's sweet, low voice sang all alone just these two lines:

"Now I lay me down to sleep,
I pray the Lord my soul to keep,"

and more than one voice responded "Amen." All that was years and years ago, but it is as vivid in my memory as if it were to-day and now. I have learned my lesson by a life-long pain, and now I never hear of a "girl who has gone to the bad," but I run to clasp her in my

Was it a Foundling?

arms and whisper, "Peace, child, peace." I have been on the board of two foundling homes and not a child is ever taken away from its mother. We take away no so=called "stigma" by taking away the child. The child is the wedge dividing the mother from her sin, and God knows it when He places any baby,

CHAPTER XX

John did not Kiss Mrs. Black's Little Girl

John had a great respect for women, and he dearly loved little girls. He showed his respect for women by being in no wise " a lady's man," in a clerical sense. Ministers seem to have an undue share of liability. Sympathy for them is subject to exaggeration. Flattery approaching a person in its true guise is recognized and held at arm's length. Not that the ministerial heart is unsusceptible. It is wary of flattery. But when flattery masks itself as sympathy, the citadel is taken by surprise. Sympathy is irresistible. It is unheralded, and treads as upon velvet. "That was a lovely sermon; it went to my heart," proceeds from a dimpled mouth radiant with smiles. The minister cannot help a certain gratitude of feeling towards one who has thus appreciated his efforts. There are more "lovely sermons" and more gratitude. After a while there are backbitings, and slander, and despair. Innocence suffers because the majority of people in the church and out of it are credulous of wrong. The more the pity!

John did not Kiss Mrs. Black's Girl

"In Christ ye are neither male nor female," wrote the apostle.

"In Christ!" But in the church and in the world, in a very vigilant and wide-awake community, we are necessarily "male and female." Society poses as a supreme bench, and its verdicts are as "unalterable as the laws of the Medes and Persians." A minister may not ignore these verdicts, be he ever so innocent. He is a "burning and a shining light." He is hung in a naughty world and is exposed to gentle breezes no less than to mighty winds. If the wind and the breeze do not extinguish his light, smoke and fog will conspire to make it dim. From my heart I sympathize with the ministers. Situated as they are "between the upper and the nether millstone," sympathy and suspicion, they are at a disadvantage.

Sympathizing with them, as I most heartily do, I always make especial friends with their wives. A minister without a wife is a ship without an anchor.

John is looking over my shoulder again and he is laughing. "You make us out rather 'weak vessels,'" he says.

"Yes, you are weak vessels," I say. "According to Scripture. You are all right yourself, John, but you know as well as I that some of them are cracked."

John did not Kiss Mrs. Black's Girl

It is too bad to record all this against a class for whom I have the highest respect, and to whom the Lord relegated the spreading of His kingdom. But, on every hand are slander, and evil-speaking, churches disrupted, the fair face of Christian ministry disfigured. "How true it is that one stain on the spotless robe of a child of Jesus is deemed blacker than the countless sins of the transgressor!" Each one of us, humble believers, is a child of Jesus, only some are on a pedestal while the rest are on the common level and hide behind one another.

As I said, "John dearly loved little girls" and he does to this day, now that the fringe of his soft hair is as white as snow peeping from under his generous skull-cap. This was one of his ways of expressing his love: A neighbor's wife called one day bringing her little Maude, a child of six years. Oh, she was pretty and winsome. Just to look at her was a festival, while to feel her soft cheek, to hold her agitated, plump little hand was—well, I cannot describe it. The child's mother appreciated it all with a mother's due license of pride, and she was never weary of "showing off" the little one in a quiet way. She meant well; she was simply thoughtless like many another happy mother, and no one could blame her who saw the child.

"Go and sit on the minister's knee, Maude

John did not Kiss Mrs. Black's Girl

darling," she said; "give him a kiss and tell him all about your new doll."

Obedient little angel that she was, Maude jumped down and ran over to John.

Did John take her on his knee and kiss ever so reverently the dimpled mouth? Not he. He took her hand respectfully and rising, said: "Let us go out and look at the roses, Maude, there are some new ones. Do you like roses and butterflies?" I heard him ask as the door closed behind them.

Away danced the child down the path like a stray bit of sunshine detached from the day's radiance.

The child's mother sat thinking. She was one of our intimate friends, innocent in heart and life, devoid of conceit and strictly effeminate of nature. She watched the two as they strolled about in the garden. Something in John's manner had struck her. Suddenly she looked me full in the face and asked, "Why did not your husband kiss the child?"

Now my first impulse might have been to evade the truth and answer, "Oh, he didn't mean anything. I guess he was thinking of something else."

But Mrs. Blank was not one to be deceived. She was frank herself and demanded frankness from others. There was an honest questioning

John did not Kiss Mrs. Black's Girl

in her eyes, a pledge of good faith, and I replied:

"John is peculiar, you know. His inclination to kiss the child, winsome little thing that she is, yielded to his principle. He often tells me that he loves little girls too well to treat them as other people do.

"John has convictions that would have made it wrong for him to take her up and kiss her. It was for her sake. What is the little girl but a little woman? Many a sweet and winning child loses neither her sweetness nor her confidence when she has grown to a young girl, and she may keep it to young womanhood. Were the world of men like my John or your William the child's sweet confidence would never be misplaced. But alas! there are men that are not good. The maiden may meet with such. And then we have the pitiless stories that bring indignation and pain to every mother's heart. John says, 'The little girl is a Shrine, something to love and reverence and hold sacred, We put our shoes from off our feet, the customs whereto cling the dust of danger, as if we were indeed on hallowed ground.' Do you understand?"

"Yes, I understand," she said, and she wore a troubled look. She was not troubled at what I had said in the way of resenting it; but at some possible mistake of her own.

John and the child came in loaded with roses.,

John did not Kiss Mrs. Black's Girl

When our guests went away the mother said, looking at John and me, "I thank you, good-bye," and John shook hands with the little one just as he did with her mother.

I don't know why we should not help one another in these simple ways. If it were not for pride, if we only loved each other better, there would be greater tolerance of one another's views. There are a thousand aimless conversations—, feeble of motive, and of what help? If we could rise above what is foolish and unhelpful, and exchange ideas upon every-day customs and topics, what changes for the better might be wrought in society! But we are afraid of "treading on one another's toes."

CHAPTER XXI

A Proposal of Marriage

I went to the study one day and found John looking perplexed, and yet not sad. In his hand was an open letter.

"What is it?" I asked, looking over his shoulder.

"It's something unusual," he answered; "read this, if you like." So I took the letter and read it while John watched my face.

Sunrise Park, Oct. 21, 18—

MR. ROBERT ALLISON:

    Dear friend:—I write to ask if you have had a serious thought as to a life-companion. If so I wish to state that I have the warmest regard for you; a regard which deepens with years and acquaintance. Should you feel a like growing regard for me, be assured that in me you would find those elements of sincere and faithful friendship which mark congenial unions. In spite of the rising color which I feel as I write, I am conscious that my heart and heaven approve a step which, on the face of it, may be somewhat startling to yourself. Trusting that you will pardon the privilege which I have claimed, and appreciate to some extent the confidence which I have reposed in you, I am your friend,

RACHEL WATERBURY.

"Well, well!" I exclaimed; "who would have thought that of Rachel Waterbury?"

A Proposal of Marriage

In his first surprise Robert Allison had brought the letter to John. The young man was a gentleman of unusual dignity, gifted physically and mentally. He had never been known to "keep company" with any lady, although his esteem for women was not concealed. As to age, he was some twenty-eight or thirty—somewhat older than the lady who had addressed him. Rachel Waterbury is already known to the reader as of lovely character, rich in good deeds and of modest mien. In her own right she had a sufficient fortune.

"Well, dear," said John, "do you see anything out of the way in this?"

"Yes," I replied, "it is all out of the way. How can any woman make such a proposal? I thought Rachel Waterbury almost perfect until now. What *can* Robert Allison think of her?"

John did not reply and I went back to my work, meditating. The more I thought of it the more I was convinced that a union between these two would be just the thing, provided it could have come about in the natural way. From feeling shocked at first, I came to tolerate the new departure, and at last to feel anxious as to a favorable outcome. There came to me glimpses of the urgent conviction which must have impelled Rachel Waterbury to pen that letter.

A Proposal of Marriage

I felt the dignified frankness of it and the sincerity of every line. No gush, no fervid revelation of passion, no silly protests of undying affection.

I may be forgiven for having watched the two the next Sunday, when I should have been thinking of the sermon. When they met, as they had done every Sabbath for years at the Sunday-school, or after church, there was a certain defined respect in the young man's manner impossible to describe. Not self-conscious in the least, and hardly with a change of color, the young lady seemed as "calm as a summer sea." "What is surging in your respective bosoms? I wondered and what are your thoughts of each other?"

The sequel was a happy one. John married the pair three months after that extraordinary proposal. And John declared that the ceremony was so impressive to him that he needed not the proof of added years to convince him it was right. Suffice it to say that this union was one of the happiest we ever knew. How could it help being such with a foundation of mutual respect verging upon reverence? From the moment he received the letter, Robert Allison said his former esteem for Rachel Waterbury ripened into an indescribable regard. His first surprise flowered into amazement at

A Proposal of Marriage

his own stupid lack of perception. It was as if he had loved her all his life.

"But what a risk for her!" I said to John. "Just think if repugnance had been in the place of esteem. It would have ruined her. It was an awful step for any woman to take."

"That was impossible," John replied. "How could any man be offended at such a letter from such a woman? It was not the flippant dash of a daring girl, nor yet the religiously sentimental outburst of a weak nature."

John had his own ways of conducting marriage ceremonies.

I used to say: "John, you are too particular. Isn't it prying of you to ask so many questions? Really sensitive persons might take offense and call you impertinent. It's their own affair if they are not congenial. All you have to do in the matter is to perform the ceremony and pocket the fee. Ten to one you will never see the couples again. They go their way and you go yours."

I used to say this to John at first. After a while I learned to think as he did. When very young couples came to him, or especially if the lady were young, he never performed the ceremony without written or verbal consent of her parents, except in those cases when he was sure consent was withheld on account of unworthy

A Proposal of Marriage

motives. He actually assisted one young couple to elope, being perfectly assured that he was justified in doing so.

Under no circumstances did he marry a couple without a private talk with each separately. More than once has he caused the marriage to be postponed and in several instances to be given up altogether.

John had a way of getting at the heart of things without effort. Confidence expanded of itself, if he but invited it. In those separate talks he learned all about the health, moral aspirations, propensities and spiritual experience of the applicant.

As to health, it was John's emphatic conviction that no man nor woman who has an immediate or remote probability of disease has any moral or physical right to marry. "Count the cost," he would say; "put into the scales present self=sacrifice against future distress and the inevitable entailment of disease upon others, and which is the heavier? It is terrible, the life=long strain upon affection; the bodily weakness is a blight upon all that makes many lives rich and fruitful. We have but to look to see. There are the moral probabilities: the history of crime in a family, the taint of bad reputation, remote or near. 'If I marry him I will reform him,' is a cheat. 'If you do not

A Proposal of Marriage

marry me, I shall go to the bad,' is an insult. 'I shall win him to faith,' thinks the Christian girl in the hopefulness of her ardent nature. This, too, is a cheat. Without mutual faith in God—in short, without a third party to the union there can be no happiness."

This is the way John argued the case and many a generous fee was returned to, or rather retained in its owner's pocket in consequence. John never once thought of the fee—that is, not till after the ceremony. He was thinking of Time's fee, which is always extorted from the careless. Not that John ignored a marriage fee when everything was clear sailing There was nothing so merry as a marriage bell. to him, when it had the true ring.

Of course, John was the spiritual adviser of many a wedded pair and he had a keen insight into many an infelicity. He was ingenious in advice and very discreet as to giving any advice at all. I do not know how it is that women are so much more willing than men, to communicate in the matter of conjugal disagreement. A man will eat his dinner in silence, light his pipe and wander down to the courthouse steps, or to his club, or to the saloon as the case may be; or he will busy himself in his newspaper (the paper upside down) and philosophize upon his situation in the privacy of his own heart. Very

A Proposal of Marriage

seldom does he communicate his sorrows to a friend.

With the partner of his sorrows it is different. She tells it all to a generous neighbor, mingling her tears with her suds, or wiping her eyes on an embroidered handkerchief, as the case may be. She is sure of sympathy, and she gets what she is sure of, with many an anathema upon the sterner sex, and a companion tear over the fact that "men are such brutes."

She finds her way to the minister's study and there pours out her soul and her husband's soul in the presence of Clarke, and D'Aubigne and Geikie, and Farrar, and Tyndall, who are staring at her in mute dismay from their seats on the book-shelves. The minister sighs; at heart he is in sympathy with the accused absent brother. But he must not give offense to his female client. Women make up two-thirds of his congregation—besides, to be courteous is his second nature. He is sorry for his complainant and he tells her so. He "hopes for the best"; "perhaps things will change"; any way, he will remember her "in his prayers."

His visitor goes away with a warm feeling towards the minister and herself. She somehow feels that the minister is on her side, though she cannot remember exactly what he said. She is "strengthened," she thinks, and she takes heart.

A Proposal of Marriage

When she meets her husband she feigns a smile. She is "ahead of him" in the minister's sympathy, she thinks. She fancies, when she next meets the minister, that he is giving her sympathetic glances.

Oh, this lack of pride on woman's part! This deplorable tendency to give oneself and one's husband quite away, without so much as a pennyworth of reserve!

John had methods of his own. For instance, Mrs. Mc Deavitt rang the bell. She seated herself in the low chair John politely offered her. She wiped her eyes, and looked imploringly at John. "Can I do anything for you?" he asked. "Are you in trouble?"

"Yes, indeed, I am in trouble!" and she burst into a Johnstown flood of tears. When the shower was over she turned her liquid eyes upon John and whimpered: "My husband isn't what he used to be."

"Oh," John said in surprise.

"No, he isn't. He is cold—and—well—I can't explain it, and I don't know as I ought to try. But he isn't what he used to be."

"Are you thinking of a divorce?" John asked, respectfully.

"A divorce!" exclaimed Mrs. Mc Deavitt. "Why, what should I do without Mr. Mc Deavitt? He's a good provider and he's good to the chil-

A Proposal of Marriage

dren, and he stands well in society. It's not that; but he isn't what he used to be, and the neighbors know it, too," and John's visitor burst into another flood of tears.

"Let me help you," John said, really sorry for the misguided woman. "Are you sure that you yourself are just what you used to be? Would you have dreamed in your halcyon days of finding fault with your husband either to his face or behind his back? Would you have sat tearfully by and heard your neighbors descant upon him and upon men in general as if they were a band of cannibals making a raid upon helpless womenfolk with intent to eat them alive? How do your neighbors know that your husband is not just what he used to be? Let me give you a bit of advice, since you have not asked it, and therefore I am not almsgiving. The next time one of your neighbors makes a remark not complimentary to your husband or to men in general, fly at them. Make as though you would tear them limb from limb. It will be a wonder to yourself, the sudden esteem in which you will hold your husband when once you have defended him. It is an inborn principle of the human heart. To defend another is to make that other a hero. Try it, my friend. If this doesn't work and your husband really goes from bad to worse——"

A Proposal of Marriage

"I'll have you to know my husband isn't bad!" exclaimed John's visitor with an earnestness that caused John to move back two steps. "He's better than you are!" and she actually laughed through her tears. Then she went home.

Good men like my John are as thick as stars, but oh, dear me, if they knew how women talk about them behind their backs! It is a shame! How can I help it though?

CHAPTER XXII

I Attend Some Other Churches

John insisted upon my attending other churches from time to time, both "as a change for you," he said, and to "get pointers" for him.

I told him that I was "afraid it wouldn't look right." It would seem as if I did not appreciate him, or that I was fickle or heretical or something. I had never seen a minister's wife attend other churches, and I was sure it would give the impression that "something was awry."

Come to think of it, however, it must be monotonous for a minister's wife to always sit in the same pew and always look interested in the preacher and the sermon, and appear to be listening to the sermon for the first time, when all the while she knows it by heart and is wishing she could go across the way and "hear that other minister everybody is talking about."

Always there is the same enforced interest and the same gray shawl and the same alpaca dress, and much the same bonnet with alterations in the trimming that everyone sees year in and year out.

I Attend Some Other Churches

It was kind of John to insist on my visiting the neighbor churches, though I do say that John's sermons were always good and interesting to me. But I learned something of the world in going about, and John was glad of the hints it gave him.

One day I strolled up the hill above the town to a little church almost out of sight of the street. It had not been built for this congregation, but was the original property of some other which had outgrown it and sold it to its present owners. The tiny edifice had been moved up the street to its present site. Inside there was a cross, like the rest of the finish high up in front, and there was no pulpit, only a raised platform. I almost expected to see the choir-boys in white emerge from somewhere and sing to us; but they had gone away, or rather the little church had gone away from them. The cross, which had been in the heart of the church in the old time, remained in its old place. To me it seemed the token of peace between churches and the "oneness" the Lord prayed might be in the possession of His universal church.

The choir of four were in their seats; there was no organist in sight. Upon the organ lay a single rose. The effect of that single rose was marvelous. No work of the florist's art, with its multiplicity of beauty, could have compared

I Attend Some Other Churches

with it. A familiar hymn was announced by the minister, and still the seat at the organ was empty. As he read the last line of the hymn the preacher turned and sat down to the instrument. A single word of information that "the organist was away and others were not familiar with the instrument" was the sole apology for this new departure in the Sunday service. After the sermon, when the closing hymn was announced, the minister again took his place at the organ, and then, rising and facing the audience, he pronounced the benediction, his coat skirt draping the organ seat behind him. There was a certain unfamiliar grace in all this that touched the finer feelings. The whole was so natural, and yet so unique, that I seemed in some new realm of ministerial responsibility.

I was very much interested and sometimes amused as I went about at the reading of "church notices." I used to wonder if the railroads would not yet announce their time-tables from the pulpit, and the hotels their prices for board and lodging, and the grocers their charge for family flour and potatoes. Picnics, mountain excursions, sewing societies and public lectures were actually announced. I remember being at a certain church and hearing the preacher read with all solemn gravity: "On Friday a fair will be held in this church, in the

I Attend Some Other Churches

south parlor, at which aprons will be sold for ten cents apiece and dish towels for five cents. In the evening beautiful booths will be ready for strangers, where three guesses at what is behind the curtains may be had for fifteen cents. Refreshments will be had for twenty-five cents, after which we shall repair to the north parlor, where the floor has been waxed for the occasion." Then followed, in the same tone of voice, the usual "Let us pray."

After the prayer came a few explanatory words to the effect that if we "would keep our young people from going astray in this age of the world the church itself must furnish recreation."

Another day I heard a church notice to the effect that "Ladies will be sold at the coming church fair to the highest bidder. What were left would be given away for ten cents apiece." Following this announcement was a word of exhortation from the preacher in a really begging tone: "We are in need of funds and some means must be used to obtain them. Strangers, one and all, are cordially invited."

I attended, one Sabbath, a church which I had been told was "not exactly evangelical." But I knew a good many of the members in a social way, so I saw no reason why I should not go there once, and John did not object. What was my surprise on entering, a trifle late, to hear

I Attend Some Other Churches

the congregation singing the dear, familiar tune—

> Nearer my God to thee, nearer to thee,
> E'en though it be a cross that raiseth me.

"There must be some mistake," I thought. "These people cannot sing about the cross and reject the One who sanctified and endeared the cross to all the world." I looked about the beautiful auditorium and saw the cross in lovely panels upon every door, and the window-casings, too. Even the stained glass was set in cross-sections and far up in the dome an angel was flying in midheaven bearing a cross half-hidden by his extended wings. "Ah," thought I, "until architecture takes on new features the story of the cross will be written in doors and windows and frescoed walls."

I was in such an unexpected devotional ecstasy that when the closing hymn was given out I was glad to sing, for I loved that hymn—

> There's a wideness in God's mercy
> Like the wideness of the sea;
> There's a kindness in His justice
> Which is more than liberty.
>
> There is no place where earth's sorrows
> Are more felt than up in heaven;
> There is no place where earth's failings
> Have such kindly judgment given.

I was so intent upon the beautiful piece that I did not notice I was singing the next verse

I Attend Some Other Churches

quite alone. I sang on with my eyes fixed upon the cross in the window—

>There is welcome for the sinner,
>And more graces for the good;
>There is mercy with the Savior,
>There is healing in his blood.

I was all unconscious of what I was doing and chimed right in when the congregation sang the next verse, which was in the book—

>For the love of God is broader
>Than the measure of man's mind,
>And the heart of the Eternal
>Is most wonderfully kind.

Forgetting everything else I was singing right on—

>There is plentiful redemption
>In the blood that has been shed,—

when some one pulled my sleeve and whispered: "You are not singing from the book.' I was conscious of an astonished rustle of hymn-books, and when I looked at the hymn before me I saw that the verses which I had been singing were left out of the hymn. My face burned and I left the church as soon as the benediction was pronounced. When I got home I had a good cry at my stupidity, and told John I would "never go to another church but our own again." I had made "a fearful blunder," I said. "The idea of my being so forgetful as to sing without

I Attend Some Other Churches

looking on the page, and to sing verses which the whole congregation besides myself knew had been left out of the book on purpose."

John smiled and said he was real glad I had "done justice to grand old Faber. The dear saint would rise up and thank me," he was sure, "for compelling that church to see that they had left out the very heart of his sublime hymn. The whole piece counts for nothing without those verses. It is like taking the heart out of a man and then bidding him live and move and save a world."

But John could not make me forget that I had been guilty of bad form or ill-breeding to mention "blood" in that connection. I have always been very careful since to stick to the text when I am singing. But it does seem strange, come to think of it now, that the church should have been singing "Nearer, my God, to thee," and yet leave out those verses that refer to the Savior by name and by his sacrifice. Of what possible meaning has the cross, separated from our sacrifice? How can a cross raise us "nearer to God" without the Christ who gave himself on the cross?

CHAPTER XXIII

Election and Reprobation

John said that "if Faber had written that hymn before the time of Cain and Abel, the two brothers would most likely have sung it together with all the enthusiasm of devotion"—that is, all but the two verses which I had sung alone at the church which was not "exactly evangelical." "Those, Abel would have sung quite by himself." Imagine Cain saying to his brother Abel, "There is total lack of reason in this religion of yours that demands blood for sacrifice. For my part I see no need. We are all sons of God, and there is that in every one of us that can lift us up without the shedding of blood. I will pay my vows to the Most High in my own way. Besides, the idea of blood is repugnant to me. It is not in good form, and I dislike the word, especially in this connection. There is my son Enoch, scarcely more than a baby yet—am I going to bring him up to think of sacrifice as necessary? I do not believe in sacrifice."

I suppose it never occurred to Cain that it was vulgar to speak of the blue blood of aristocracy, nor to refer to his own father as belong-

Election and Reprobation

ing to blood of the very first water. He could speak of the royal blood, which, flowing through his own veins, stood always between him and the more common types, such as dwelt down in the land of Nod and elsewhere. Cain realized that it was different, this royal blood which he felt in himself, from the blood of sacrifice which in some unaccountable way made all men royal. The one was a legacy coming to him in a natural sort of way, lifting him above the meaner sort; the other, being outside of inheritance, was a gift, which, accepted by such as could boast little lineage, insured to them an aristocracy imperial. This last, being quite out of the natural, it was considered inelegant to refer to, and Cain grew very wroth with his brother Abel for having any faith at all in such a tenet.

Cain and Abel offer their sacrifices to-day "in the field," and Cain would slay his brother—or rather he would destroy his altars, eradicating, as he thinks, the last trace of a belief in imparted royal blood. Still pedigree manifests itself, and we see those about us who have come of poor stock suddenly endowed with noble extraction, claiming descent from a long line of ancestors as lordly as they were illustrious.

As to sacrifice—personal sacrifice for another —which Cain would have nothing of, there was his mother. He loved her, but he never thought

Election and Reprobation

of her as a sacrifice. He could see her growing gray with anxiety for him, and "working her fingers off" in helping his father at farming, that they all might have enough to eat under the new order. "But that was natural," he would have answered, if Abel had ventured an allusion. We worship the "natural" while abhorring the spiritual—that part or principle of which the natural is but a prophecy. If, by the sacrifice of one, bread for the natural is provided, why feign surprise that, by the sacrifice of another, bread for the spiritual is provided?

Speaking of Cain and Abel, I remember something John said once about "election and reprobation." Seeing that Cain was awry with the present system of theology, that he was sleepless and blaming the fates for locating him in that particular part of the country, the Creator spoke to the young man and said: "What is the matter?"

Cain's reply is not given, but it must have been something connected with election and reprobation, or else God would not have spoken those words which decided the question of "free will," forever.

"If thou doest well shalt thou not be accepted?" That was election. "And if thou doest not well, sin lieth at the door." That was reprobation.

"Why art thou wroth, Cain? Why is thy

Election and Reprobation

countenance fallen?" It is said that God looks at the heart. This is no doubt true, but he also looks at the face, or perchance he has no need of gazing at the heart, since he may read the heart in the face. It was an early lesson in physiognomy. Cain's face had changed. It had "fallen." And God took notice. It was the first face in the "rogue's gallery." I named this chapter "Election and Reprobation" because I should have so little to say about it. I got that idea from John. He says the less you say about contended points the better for your cause. It is not so much in the "point at issue" as in the contention which the point gives license to. Religion has not given rise to the disputations which those who cavil have claimed. It is the spirit of contention in a man which too often makes him the advocate of a doctrine. It is not that his whole soul is in his doctrine; his whole soul is in contention. Good men have been so swayed by it, at the same time denying contention, that it became a matter of life and death with them as to whether their theories were adopted or not. Hence the valiant army of martyrs has had its recruits. Men have died of contention, fancying themselves martyrs to religion. It was contention, not Christian religion, that condemned the soul of Origen "to everlasting damnation for having expressed

Election and Reprobation

hopes of the final pardon of sinners." Origen was not free from contention, albeit he was a martyr to religion. Why need he have contended for his belief in the final pardon of sinners, since those self-same sinners would martyr him? The last day would have vindicated the cause of sinners and left his opponents unpardoned by the verdict of their own theory.

CHAPTER XXIV
The Tuttle Family

John came home one day looking so tired I thought he must be sick, but on second thought I concluded he was thinking about the Tuttle family down in Cades Canyon. He had driven the children over in the afternoon "just to give them an outing," he said, but I knew his real errand was to see how Ben Tuttle was getting along. Ben wasn't poor. He was on a good salary, though he worked hard. He kept the outlets clear and the main pipes in order for the water companies, and was obliged to stand in cold water up to his waist for hours at a time.

Somebody had suggested to him a year or so before that a little spirits of some sort would keep him from taking cold. It was the old story. He soon came to drink enough to keep two men warm. His wife found out about the drink and quite naturally took to scolding. I say "quite naturally," for when a woman feels hopeless in any cause she scolds as a last resort. I scold, myself, sometimes, and am ashamed of it afterwards, though John says I "needn't be, for when a great many women scold in concert they

The Tuttle Family

effect reformations in society." So I suppose it is only individual scolding that is really ill-bred and useless.

Ben told me afterward that if Mrs. Tuttle had but sent him some hot coffee two or three times a day it would have helped him to let the drink alone. I have noticed that transgressors are apt to blame someone else for such advance as they make in their besetting sin. But I do not read anywhere that God ever excused any man for sinning by telling him that his "brother or his wife ought to have done differently." And so I told John one day. John only answered that he supposed "God must think a great many things to himself which he wouldn't dream of telling us."

I had often seen the Tuttle family. Mrs. Tuttle was a real pretty woman, but so slovenly I wondered her husband ever came home at all. She was sick a good deal and the children managed as best they could. After a while people became interested in them on account of Ben's drink, and scarcely a day passed that they were not visited by a temperance committee. They would sit down and sigh, or take up the baby and say "Poor thing!" If Ben Tuttle happened to come in, they looked at him reproachfully and asked him if he knew "how sick his poor wife was."

The Tuttle Family

Once I saw a woman sniff at his coat which was hanging behind the door, evidently to see if she could "smell a bottle." But Ben knew better than to bring bottles home. He hid them behind the rocks down in the canyon.

One year, about Christmas, Mrs. Tuttle suddenly "took religion," as she termed it, and then the household economy was more than ever neglected. Well=meaning women came early in the morning to sing and pray and talk. They had not got far enough in life's lesson to understand that religion consists more in doing than in saying.

When Tuttle came home to dinner, tired and wet and hungry, he expected something to eat, of course. But what did he find? A dirty baby asleep in the middle of the kitchen floor, hens walking around it pecking at the scraps it held in its little closed fist, the breakfast dishes unwashed in the sink, and covered with flies, and his wife sitting on the side of the bed reading "Woe unto him that putteth the bottle to him, and giveth his neighbor drink."

If she had turned to Proverbs and read the vivid description of the wise woman who "riseth while it is yet night and giveth food to her household," results might have been different. She never looked up when her husband came in, but kept on praying and reading, hoping to

The Tuttle Family

convince him. The oldest girl was trying to get dinner. A piece of steak was steaming and oozing in a vain attempt to fry itself in the milk-warm skillet; and in a kettle were some potatoes simmering beneath a gallon of water—long since "done" in their dirty jackets.

I saw this picture several times, and am not exaggerating it. Ben looked at his wife and then at the baby, drove the hens out and—did he scold? No, indeed! Men pride themselves that they never scold. But he did what was almost as bad; he boxed little Tom's ears, kicked the cat that was licking out the breakfast plates in her blind desire to be doing something, and walked out of doors.

Then Mrs. Tuttle and the oldest girl began to cry, and the way looked darker than ever. John persuaded Ben to wear rubber tights when he was in the water as an aid in preventing chills, but he drank all the same and the family went on praying and crying and eating irregular meals.

A strange sort of people who called themselves "Christian Scientists" got to arguing with Tuttle one day. He told us about it. They said there "wasn't any such thing as whisky; that he just imagined it was good, and that it was imagination that was driving him and his family wild."

The Tuttle Family

"Don't you see," they said, "there isn't any evil in the world but in man's imagination? Here's the orthodox Bible to prove it: 'And God saw that the imagination of man was only evil continually.' So you mustn't believe there is any good in drink; really there is neither good nor evil in it, and you can leave off your habits if you just think of something else."

"Well," returned Tuttle, "it's a pretty reviving kind of imagination sometimes when a man is cold and hungry. Ought to be cheaper, don't you think? The idea of a tariff on imagination!"

I worried a good deal about the family and so did a great many other women who belonged to the church. We used to drop in and sympathize with Mrs. Tuttle, and try to do the work up a little, just to show her how it ought to be done. But it made Ben so angry when he came home, we had to give it up. Mrs. Tuttle didn't like it neither—" the neighbor women peering around into her closets, and winking at one another when they found a particularly dirty corner, or a wasteful platter of scraps in the cupboard." Yes, indeed! I worried, but John didn't. He never worried about anything. He said " God hadn't lost sight of the Tuttle family, and He would probably see that they had a chance to touch the hem of His garment yet if the crowd of meddlesome committees, that lacked

The Tuttle Family

judgment, would fall back long enough." John remembered the Tuttles in family prayers every morning, not putting God in mind, as though He were forgetting them, nor nagging at Him in an impatient sort of way, but emphasizing "Thy will be done," as if that particular "will" was all the world needs to set it right.

Well, this takes us up to the time John came home looking so tired. After a while he took the Bible down and read how Peter, in his zeal, without knowledge, drew his sword and cut off somebody's right ear. And then he told me that he had been over to Cades Canyon and found brothers Goodsoul and Rightenough there, arguing with Tuttle. They had gone down to where he was working in the water and attacked him with what the Bible says about "damnation" and "better put a knife to thy throat" and "without are drunkards," etc., hurling all sorts of terrible insinuations at him; and there stood Ben in the water shivering with cold and anger. His "right ear" had been cut off by Peter's officious sword. He didn't know whether "to commit suicide or lay his well-meaning visitors out on the rocks," he said.

This lack of Christian courtesy and good judgment on the part of those men was what made John so tired. He says he thinks such passages as they had selected are to be "read in a tender,

The Tuttle Family

pitying tone, with entire lack of assertion, which would do away with their seeming harshness and make a man feel sorry that his sin had driven the Father to inflict pain on His children, which could only be equaled by what He himself felt on their account."

A week or two after this John went over again and stopped at the house a minute. There he found a Salvation Army woman telling the children stories while she cleaned them up and made Mrs. Tuttle more comfortable. John said he stayed around the yard examining the cow and hens, just to see how things were going. The whole family liked John, and he felt that he was in no eavesdropper's shoes.

While the stranger was at work she sang rollicking songs that soon made Mrs. Tuttle stop groaning, and then laugh—the first time she had laughed in a year. Not the words, but the tune was so rollicking. John said if he had had the blues himself he would have smiled.

"I'm a soldier, as you see," was sung to the tune of "So early in the morning," and "The Salvation Army will conquer the world," to the tune of "I'm a man you don't meet every day." John could see that the little woman was conquering that household, and so he wandered down to the water pipes.

Long before he could see Ben he heard

TELLING THE CHILDREN STORIES WHILE SHE CLEANED THEM
UP AND MADE MRS. TUTTLE COMFORTABLE.

The Tuttle Family

somebody singing, moving along in the brush toward the spot where Tuttle was. The tune was, "Now isn't it funny they don't?" and the words were the same we often heard on the corner where the torches stop in the evening right in front of Peterson's cigar stand:

> "For years I have followed the devil around
>   But Satan and I are out.
> He promised me pleasure but none I have found,
>   So Satan and I are out.
> He once held a mortgage upon my poor soul,
> But Christ paid it off and made me quite whole,
> And off from my heart the burden did roll—
>   And Satan and I are out.

When the Captain got opposite Tuttle he stopped and passed the time of day and inquired if he wasn't cold. "I was a minute ago," Ben answered, "but that singing of yours made me forget. Do you come this way often?"

"Oh, yes," his visitor answered, "when I have an errand."

John knew the "errand" had been done with the singing. It was dinner time, and the two walked up to the house, John behind them. The visitor began to sing again, not in a rollicking tone this time, but in a sweet voice that fluttered up into the treetops and then trailed along in the dried leaves, or rustled in the wild grape vines:

The Tuttle Family

I'll trust thee noo dear Savior, I'll trust Thee as I go,
Oh, I would live and seek thy love, nae ither wud I know.
Ye've ta'en the burden of my sins, ye've dune a heap for me,
Oh, take my heart dear Jesus, its a' I hae tae gae.

John said he didn't even stop to speak to the Tuttles. They did not seem to need him that day, and he came home looking so happy! —as if he were one with some sweet secret.

Now, I never admired the operations of the Salvation Army. They seem to be so flippant with solemn things, and they shock refined people with their noise and lack of good taste. But John says: "We nice, polished folks mustn't put out our hands to 'steady this ark of the Lord.' Better to make the ground smoother, grade the track a little, and the mysterious secrets of the Almighty will be taken care of."

He attends their meetings sometimes, and once when they were mobbed by the town roughs an egg came plump against his back. John told me afterwards there was such a "rush of perfect peace into his soul that he could have wished the pelting prolonged." He heard someone say, "Bear ye one another's burdens," and looked behind and around him, but nobody was speaking save the Captain, in red, who was saying: "Inasmuch as ye have done it unto one of the least of these."

The Tuttle Family

I always thought that "Bear ye one another's burdens" meant to go and sit by the sick, and carry them jelly and flowers, and attend funerals, and be sympathizing with people in distress generally. But John says the text has had a new meaning to him ever since he felt the explosion of that egg on his shoulder, which was meant for the speaker's face.

Well, the Tuttle family were won by the Salvationists, and of course Ben left off the drink.

CHAPTER XXV

Company to Dinner

We had invited Judge Rich and his family to dinner. Judge Rich was a prominent member of our church, well-to-do and highly respected in the community. Between him and John a friendship had existed for a long time. This was a marvel to me—they were so dissimilar. They were always differing in opinion, yet so good-naturedly that neither took offense.

Just as we were seated at table, and I was pushing up the baby's high chair, we heard a knock at the side door. Nancy came in to say that, "a tramp wanted to know if he could do anything to pay for his dinner."

"Certainly, certainly," answered John, "see if he needs to wash, and bring me his name."

Nancy returned to say that he "was neat enough, though threadbare," and that his name was "Archibald Frye."

"Ask Mr. Frye to come in," said John, making room for the stranger at his left. The tramp entered, somewhat embarrassed, but he was put at his ease by John's cordial manner

Company to Dinner

and hearty introduction to the whole party. It was as if he had been expected, and John was not one to ignore courtesy, though his guest was a tramp.

Judge Rich winced a bit, and his wife colored a little. I, used to my husband's ways, could but smile at his courage. Madam Grundy had seated herself, as unannounced as this tramp, at our table. As usual, she demanded respectful hearing. John was always more deaf to her remarks than ordinary people are—in fact, paid no attention to her. I was almost sorry for our guests and wished, very secretly, that "Mr. Frye" had not happened to drop in.

John, after grace, carved the roast, and attended to the duties pertaining to mine host with more than his usual good cheer. Conversation was lively and our guests forgot their momentary annoyance. Topics of the day were freely discussed, and John led so adroitly that he had beguiled an opinion from the tramp before the rest of us knew what he was about. The tramp proved himself intelligent, and, from some timid remarks on the tariff, he came to an earnest discussion with Judge Rich on the outcome of the present hard times.

John sent me one of those telegraphic communications out of the depths of his blue eyes, so common between us, and I was more than

Company to Dinner

amused at the turn things had taken. Dinner over, the whole party retired to the parlor, with the exception of the tramp, who excused himself and went out. John followed him to the door where he stood talking with him for a few minutes, when the two shook hands cordially, as if they had been old friends, and parted. The tramp went down the street in search of "a job," no doubt, and John went into the parlor.

"Well," said Judge Rich, "you astonish me by your hospitality! If you continue this thing, John, mark the words of an old lawyer, you will be overrun with tramps. In such times as these one cannot be too reserved. It is true we ought to feed the hungry, and clothe the naked, but there is danger in too much freedom—though I must confess this latest tramp was no disgrace to your table. I believe you knew him, now, didn't you, or you would have been less cordial?"

"No," replied John, "I did not know him. It would have been the same had he been clothed in rags and with the look of a criminal. As long as we spread a table the destitute, from whatever cause, are welcome. I often wish they would come again, and often we invite them, but strange as it may seem the same face has never appeared at our door twice."

Company to Dinner

"Don't you think," continued the Judge, "that vagrancy is encouraged by your methods? Instead of a beggar feeling his true position, as it really is, a mean and degraded one, you bid him feel at home and help himself as if he deserved distinction. Now we discriminate at our house, as most of our church people do. We never turn a beggar away, but when a tramp comes along my wife sets out the scraps on the backdoor steps. The idea of feeding a tramp from china, and seating him beside your own children! There are always remnants left from yesterday's meals which would otherwise be wasted. They are good enough for tramps, and are eaten by them with avidity, too, unless they happen to be full. Coffee for them is as good from a tin cup as coffee from a lacquered bowl with a mouthpiece."

Here I remembered that I had taken a mustache cup from the sideboard for Mr. Frye, out of respect for John. I did a great many things out of respect for John for which I deserve no other credit. I think I should be a Christian out of respect for John if for no other reason. The fact that a thing pleased John made that very thing the one of all others which I was determined to do. To please him I would sew an occasional button on the neck of a tramp's

Company to Dinner

shirt, and for the same reason pass the same tramp coffee in a mustache cup instead of a cracked bowl.

"Judge Rich," I said, "I used to feed the tramps on the backdoor step, or give them a piece to put in their pockets, till one day it happened to be a big overgrown boy with a coat too short in the sleeves and trousers too short in the legs. His freckles had not all faded, and his downy beard appeared on his sunburned face in a manner that appealed to my heart. He looked, generally speaking, very much like our Harry when he returned last summer from his tramp in the mountains. I thought of our Harry and felt ashamed for having offered this boy food out of doors as if he were a dog, and I took him right in. It was for no other reason than that I loved Harry. Before he was gone he was shaved with Harry's razor, his coat sleeves let down at the wrist, and a bright necktie adjusted, almost affectionately, at his unhandsome throat, just in front of, and hiding a prominent 'Adam's apple.' Now, don't think for a moment, Judge, that I loved that awkward stranger boy. I do not deserve credit, for it was the thought of our own dear tramp, Harry, which moved me. I am sure John and I don't love tramps just because they are tramps. It is for

Company to Dinner

somebody's sake that we make room for them at the table."

"In My name," said John. "The Master knew the nature God had given us when He told us to give the cup of water in His name. For His sake, because we love Him, we will do a thousand things for them we do not love—just as my wife, for the sake of our boy Harry, caused the boy tramp to be made comfortable and almost goodlooking. Half of Christendom are looking for the Christ to come again. I, too, look for Him. I may seat nine unworthy ones, tramps, at my table; the tenth may be the Lord himself; for did He not say, 'Inasmuch as ye have done it unto one of the least of these ye have done it unto Me?' We look for the Lord to come in the clouds of heaven. I would not miss inviting Him to come in before that last appearing, nor set stale pieces for Him on the backdoor steps."

"Well," answered the Judge, "I think you carry things to an extreme. These tramps will never thank you for it. I always notice that they go away from our house with a sullen, dissatisfied look, as if they would have had something more, or, indeed, all we have. In most cases they are self=made tramps. They might have saved something out of former wages. There is that family on D street we were speaking of,

Company to Dinner

you know. They are foolish; they do not know how to take care of money when they have it. And now they are destitute, and I saw you, John, leave a basket of provisions at their door yesterday. I think it's mistaken kindness, and you'll excuse me for saying it. That man has always been on good wages until now, and he ought to have saved for a rainy day. It seems as though such people will never learn. And they expect us, who save, and plan for the future, to support them as soon as they are out of work. I have no patience with them. They buy the choicest cut of meat, and the finest brand of flour when they are in luck, and starve, but for us, when they are out of luck."

John smiled sadly, while he replied: "Too bad, too bad! But, Judge, we read that God said far back in the time of Moses, without a why or wherefore, 'The poor shall never cease out of the land.' Like a refrain Jesus took up the words and sent them down to the church, 'The poor ye have always with you.' It is a simple fact, like spring and summer. We are prone to exclaim with the old prophet, 'Surely they are poor, they are foolish.' They *are* foolish, it is true, many and many a time. Who of us were not foolish if God himself were the judge. As to feeding the tramp on the back doorstep——"

Company to Dinner

Here a gentleman called for Judge Rich and the conversation was closed. In thinking it all over since, I am not sure that we were never imposed upon. And yet, to this day, we always feed the tramps, and if it is mealtime they sit at the table.

CHAPTER XXVI

Earth to Earth, Ashes to Ashes, Dust to Dust, in Sure and Certain Hope of the Resurrection

I was never in the habit of attending funerals; indeed, I had never been to one in all my married life, nor had I looked upon a dead face except in those cases, before mentioned, when the necessity of "neighborliness" demanded it.

One day the daughter of a friend died, and John urged me to attend the funeral "just to show my sympathy." The family were not members of our church, and a neighboring minister conducted the services. I went, just to please John, and I have been sorry ever since. The whole hour was a torture to me, and if to me, what must it have been to the bereaved family!

When I got there a few of the neighbors were already seated. Two or three of them were sighing, and even sobbing loud enough to be heard through the house. I knew these women were in no wise related to the family, nor had they ever been intimate. I have learned since that

Hope of the Resurrection

there are people, especially elderly women, who make a practice of attending funerals and making a show of sorrow which they do not feel at all, and then go home to criticise the actual mourners, and tell how this one did not "seem to feel it any," and that one "took it to heart dreadfully," and the other one "actually never shed a tear," and "there wasn't a looking-glass in the house turned face to the wall," and "the corpse didn't look at all natural," and "the coffin was only stained pine when they could have afforded better," etc., etc.

As I said, I was a little early, in time to see the minister walk sadly in as if he, too, had lost a friend. He shook hands in a melancholy way with each of the family, and then he whispered with several of them, loud enough for all to hear, seeming to elicit points as to age, and sickness, and preparation for death. Then the service began in a dirge—I think it was "Sister thou wast mild and lovely." Now that hymn was never a favorite of mine. There is something abnormally sad about it, sung as it so often is while the sod falls like a muffled knocking on the coffin-lid at the bottom of the grave. It has too much of the painful reminiscence, and too little of Faith's uplifting.

Besides, it is sung inconsistently sometimes. "Gentle as the summer breeze," "Pleasant as

Earth to Earth, in Sure and Certain

the air of evening," are made applicable in the excitement of the sad moment to some veritable scold who in her lifetime was well known to be anything but "pleasant" and "gentle." But to go back to the funeral.

After the dirge the minister prayed. He told the Lord how much "this bereaved family had loved this dear one; the form that now lies before them cold in death." He mentioned the fact, while he sobbed, that "their hearts were all bleeding, and how they would miss her at breakfast, and dinner, and supper," and how they could remember that "Jesus wept" and how they would all "meet again bye-and-bye, after all these parting scenes were over." It was the most curious prayer I had ever heard at that time, though since then I have listened to many a one like it. We have all heard them, these funeral prayers, fashioned into a probe wherewith to tear apart the partially healed wound. It is done for effect upon the listeners, to make the particular hour stand out in life's wilderness like a pillar of salt, a monument of congealed tears to commemorate a backward glance at devastated homes.

When the prayer was done everybody was crying audibly, almost wailing—and how could they help it, especially the dead girl's mother? Then they sang again and the grief grew more

Hope of the Resurrection

still, only to burst forth with greater intensity as the sermon advanced.

The minister took for his text, "I know that the child will not return to me." And then he went on in almost a repetition of his prayer, tearing open the wound with pitiless hand, laying bare the arteries of bereavement, sharpening the grief, and making more poignant the sting of it.

The sound of crying increased, and the preacher seemed to take heart at the sound, leaving not so much as a fig leaf of present comfort to cover so naked a sorrow. The comfort was in the far future, on the "other side of Jordan, where the waters cease to roll." There was no lifting of soul and body above the grief no gilding of despair with the gold leaf of everlasting reparation—everlasting because covering the past, present and future of human life with the radiance of God's own sorrows. It is true, the minister did attempt to comfort the family with the assurance that the dear one was "better off," and "we wouldn't have her back if we could," and many such platitudes so familiar to one who makes a practice of attending funerals. These platitudes came in as an afterthought. It was as though the preacher had suddenly remembered that he had not discharged his whole duty if he left them out.

Earth to Earth, in Sure and Certain

With the air of one who is satisfied that he has preached a "powerful funeral sermon," the minister then proposed that "the casket be opened so that the friends of the departed may take a last look at the face that is cold in death." I was indignant, and left the room. I suppose it was thought that I was overcome by my feelings, as were the rest. And so I was. But I did not care to feel so much pain at the mere abnormal instinct of a man who lacked the refinement of personal forgetfulness.

And yet this minister, and those present, had been accustomed, all their lives, to speak of "the Angel of Death." They had thought of death always as "a happy release," and when the last hour was mentioned, *remotely*, it was always with an upward glance to heaven and an expression of resignation on their not unhappy faces. Now that the last hour had actually come, and they were sitting with it, how different was their view, apparently! Now that, according to their previous faith, one of the family had been " taken to heaven to be happy forevermore," there was only sorrow. And they all put on black. They would wear the mourning indefinitely; those who were the sorriest would wear it a long, long time. Those a little less sorry would wear it half as long; and those who

Hope of the Resurrection

were scarcely sorry at all would don their habitual garments in a few days.

It was as if the dear one were lost, instead of being with the Lord. Heathen people of whose funeral rites I have read can scarcely seem more desolate, expecting no everlasting life to come. "Earth to earth, dust to dust, ashes to ashes" was emphasized, while the sound of tears muffled the "sure and certain hope.' John always said it seemed to him like a mockery of faith. It is no wonder that the unbelieving world taunt us in our grief and say: "You do not believe. You are not sure."

When the minister spoke of the child being "better off" and "at rest" he did it with such a wail in his voice and choking in his throat that his words had no force.

I told John I would never attend another funeral, not if I lived to be eighty. But I kept my resolution in about the same way we all do—I did go again. It was years afterwards, at the death of the only child of Rachel Waterbury and Robert Allison. I shall never forget it, and if I live myself long enough to stand with breaking heart above my dead, I shall recall that funeral sermon and John's face while he preached it. John never did believe in death as "an angel." Nor is death, in his opinion, a

Earth to Earth, in Sure and Certain

"happy release" to anyone, save as age or suffering makes it so. We all cling to life, in spite of faith in some better life. The veriest saint we know would avert the translation until some other day, and when the inevitable end comes he turns his face to the wall and sighs in forced submission, while his friends, misunderstanding him, call it resignation. Death is the "King of Terrors," the last, most dreaded "enemy," unless perchance we are morbid. And God would have it so, for has He not told us in His infinite compassion that the "last enemy" shall himself be subject to death?

"Jesus wept," not because His friend had died, for He knew that in a day he would be raised again and be as though he had not died. It was thought of all earth's agony, combined with heaven's grief, both inevitable, that moved the Christ to tears. And who shall say that He was not thinking of his Father? "The chastisement of our grief was upon him." Not only our grief was His, but the chastisement of it, the correction that would bring us out of it, the resurrection that would restore.

But to go back to the funeral. There was silence long and deep, as if words were dead, and then "Rock of ages, cleft for me," was sung as only John himself can sing it. "Thy riven side" suggested the *lesser* pain of riven human

Hope of the Resurrection

hearts, and when he came to the closing stanza, "When I soar to worlds unknown," it seemed as if we all went with him and were safely housed without any sorrows to speak of. There was little allusion to the great grief that all knew was only too keen; breaking hearts were not lacerated by unnecessary friction, the vacant chair and the empty place at the hearthstone were left to plead their own cause. And the sermon—how can I describe it? I cannot recall the words of it, but the spirit of it, the subtle, permeating essence, like some rare aroma, fills all the house where I am sitting whenever I am near a great sorrow. "Human grief" and "breaking human hearts" receded. John's text was that one which has more moved the world than any other, that one which is like a jewel upon the forehead of God whenever we look towards Him—"For God so loved the world that he gave his only begotten Son." Rachel Waterbury told me afterwards that she thought not once of her own grief while John was speaking, although it had seemed too great for her to bear till then. She could only think of the Father and of His great yearning to lift the world above its grief, seeing no way to keep us from perishing with the weight of it but by giving His only begotten Son. Out of the dire necessity that forced Him to give His Son for the life of the

Earth to Earth, in Sure and Certain

world, sprang the Light of the world to illumine the darkness of the grave—His grave and ours, with the radiance of the resurrection. And had the Father no heart to be broken, as no human heart can be broken, with the poignancy of grief? And He was alone—alone, as no human heart can be alone! No tear did the world shed in sympathy with the Father bereft of His Son, not that His Son might have life, but that a dead world might have it! And had the Son no heart to bleed that He must give His life a ransom for many lives? If God so loved the world that He gave His only begotten Son, did not Christ even so love the world? *One* were they in love, and *one* in the mightiest sorrow that earth and heaven ever knew. What else does it mean, that testimony of the prophet concerning the One who gave himself— "Surely he hath borne our griefs and carried our sorrows?" He hath borne them, lifted them up, taken them upon himself. Because the world would not let go of its sorrows, but seemed to be one with them, inseparable, the Holy One lifted both, the heart and its sorrows.

I had never dreamed before of the possibility of suffering with the Father, of the privilege which the world has, blood-bought, of sympathizing with Him who bore our sorrows and is bearing them still.

Hope of the Resurrection

When they sang there was no sobbing, but a subdued silence as if there was a Personal Presence, Grief, with distinct Holy Body in the room.

<blockquote>There is no place where earth's sorrows
Are more felt than up in heaven</blockquote>

found its way into every heart in the room, I am sure, with a new and tender assurance.

And there was no sound of crying at the last. It was as it should be. Faith leaped the distance and rested in "sure and certain hope." It was as though the moment had come in advance of its time, when "God shall wipe away all tears." In some indescribable way I felt that a time will surely come when the world may wipe away the grief of God.

In the full confidence of faith, always his own, John lifted his eyes from the grave and said:

"*In sure and certain hope of the resurrection.*"

www.ingramcontent.com/pod-product-compliance
Lightning Source LLC
Chambersburg PA
CBHW031814230426
43669CB00009B/1133